The Fatal Ride of Hannah McQuade

and Other Stories of Love, Deceit and Murder in Your Hometown

by Karen Wisniewski

ISBN 978-1-943842-89-6

1. History.
2. Stories.

Correspondence and comments:
goralka@fastmail.fm

Printed in the United States of America
First Printing: Fall 2015

This book is dedicated to my mom and dad
John and Jeanne Wisniewski

Contents

Acknowledgments

I may not have written this book without my sister Laura (Wisniewski) Lessnau's promise to edit it and make me look good.

Thank you to my husband Mike Ball and daughter Caroline Mrowka for their support. Thank you to the Dearborn Historical Museum, the volunteers, and especially curator Jack Tate for the photos and materials that give life to these stories. I also thank the following people for their support and/or assistance and if I have neglected to mention anyone I am truly sorry.

Arlene Thomas Davis, Pat Gee, Gail Hershenzon, Pat Ibbotson, Wesley Knoch, Laura Lessnau, Muriel Lobb and her cousin Elaine Arnold, Museum Guild of Dearborn, L. Glenn O'Kray, Isamay Osborn, Donna Schwartz, Nancy Taylor, Jim Toms, and Alex Wisniewski.

The information, illustrations, photos and sketches in this book were obtained and derived from a variety of research materials including historical records and books, atlases and maps, personal sketches, family histories, family albums, newspapers, journals, interviews, on line databases and library materials.

Introduction

I started researching these true tales many years ago. Any time I spoke about them to friends or family, someone would inevitably say, "You should write these down and tell these stories."

Every town, every locale and every family has its secrets. My mother's side of the family's lore begins with the first of our people to come to America in 1896. John Drobot, my great grandfather, came to earn money for his family back in Poland. He worked for one year. The night he was planning to return to Poland, with his boat ticket and savings in his pocket, he stopped in a tavern in New York to celebrate with his friends. But he never made it to the boat; he was robbed and killed in an alley. Folks in his small Polish village had no money to ship his body home for burial so his remains most likely lie in a potter's field somewhere in New York.

My father's side is not without its mysteries. My great aunt Vera and her husband split up during World War II. She was raising their two small boys and living in an apartment above my great grandfather's beergarden in Hamtramck. When my great grandfather Stan Wisniewski died, Vera's ex-husband appeared, apparently believing he could step in and run the business. Imagine his dismay when he found Vera had a new beau and was pregnant. After a terrible argument, Vera "accidentally" fell down the stairs and she and the unborn child died. No one was prosecuted and the family didn't speak of it as being a murder, except for my Busia who never told a lie in her life. Vera's boys grew up, farmed out by their father to be mostly raised by his relatives.

Murders, robberies, jealous relatives, stolen inheritances, and tragic accidents. History tends to repeat itself. Human nature being what it is, we can hardly hope that things will ever change.

Technology does change however, and advances in science, particularly forensic science change the way we are able to investigate our world and gain knowledge. We now look more closely at these kinds of criminal incidents, and we solve mysteries with the tiniest shreds of evidence.

When I researched the history of this area from before statehood, these stories just naturally appeared in record books, history books, diaries and journals, newspapers, family lore, legends and of course, cemeteries.

I hope you enjoy reading them and, if nothing else, I hope it sparks your curiosity to research mysteries in your own family and hometown.

- Karen Wisniewski

Introduction

By Karen Krepps, Ph.D.

As volunteers working together in the archives of the Dearborn Historical Museum since the spring of 2013, Karen and I complement and enhance one another's interests and abilities. Although her background is law enforcement and mine is archaeology, we found that we shared several common interests that include a passion for historical research. In working together, we continually learn from each other. To say the least, it has been inspirational, almost magical, to watch Karen research and dig into the archival files as she follows trails into the past. Since she began her work in the archives in 2008, she has helped countless individuals coming to the archives for historical information. Her knowledge of the records available has never ceased to amaze me – she knows "where the bodies are buried." She used her knack for storytelling to encapsulate information from public records, family accounts, and the archives of the Dearborn Historical Museum to share the accounts of some of the City's unsolved crimes, and other little-known events.

Karen Krepps, Ph.D.
Archaeologist and Archivist

Pictured are Gus Knoch with his two small sons Clinton and Hazen in front of the conservatory.

CHAPTER 1

Tragedy in Springwells

n the City of Dearborn, there exists no other place as unique as its southeast section. Ranging from the days of the pioneers to the present time, that area has undergone the most extensive and permanent changes.

The Ford Rouge Steel Plant, the most comprehensive and largest industrial complex in the world, was built here and was up and running by the 1920s when the area was known as Springwells. The coke ovens, mills, the dredged channel in the Rouge River, the assembly lines, the many gates and parking lots, railways and offices were contained in a mile wide and one and a half mile long piece of property. The plant changed the land it stood on forever. And around it, residential neighborhoods sprung up, low-rent apartments and flats were built practically on top of each other. Small businesses, restaurants, and places of worship were wedged in along the main streets. Roads, bridges and underpasses were constructed to accommodate the tens of thousand of workers needed to run the plant.

What was there before Henry Ford built this wonder of the 20th century?

First it was natural and untouched land, with woods and dozens of streams and creeks draining into the Rouge River. There were nearly impassable wooded areas, as well as swamps created from natural springs in the area. Aboriginal peoples lived here, seasonally, and then routinely passed through but not before burying their dead in an enormous sand ridge on the border of the Rouge River where it emptied into the Detroit River. French farm dwellings came next, with their homes always having frontage on the Rouge. A shipbuilding yard was created in a pond that is now in Woodmere cemetery. After many wars, and after many flags had flown above the city of Detroit, the area called Springwells, became the sole domain of the white man. Particularly, German settlers favored the area in the1850s. Single lane dirt roads and hand-hewn wooden bridges appeared. Farms and grazing pastures were carved out, and wells were dug. Picket fences, barns and stables were built, and gardens and orchards were planted by the residents. The community thrived.

This is the only known photo of Gus Knoch's beautiful mansion on Fort Street about 1910. It has long since been razed. Knoch family lore asserts that the home was designed by the Detroit architectural firm of Smith, Hinchman and Grylls.

The Knoch family certainly found their niche in the Springwells area of south Dearborn. Christian Knoch uprooted his family from Germany and settled on Dix Avenue, west of Lonyo. A proud and frugal German man, he had four sons. The Knoch family worked the land and found that the products that sold the best were flowers and garden vegetables. Their whole farm, a long narrow strip with their home on Dix, was dedicated to onions, cabbages, turnips and flowers, especially bulb root flowers. In the Detroit City Directory of 1877, Christian Knoch is listed as a florist.

The Knochs would appear to have nothing but happiness and prosperity in store for them, but the bad luck this family faced began in 1879.

Christian Knoch, the family patriarch, was kicked to death by his horse out in the barn early one morning. Contradicting stories described him as being discovered in the barn with two savage head wounds and was carried to his bed. Other accounts say Christian was injured and crawled back to the house for help. Either way, he died a day later. Neighbors questioned why the family horse, a very old and gentle horse would suddenly become so ornery as to lash out at its beloved owner, when it was never known to have hurt anyone before.

The bad luck continued. The oldest of Christian Knoch's sons, Charles, disappeared one day and never returned. He was supposedly going out hunting. His dog returned home without him. A diligent search was made, but no sign of Charles Knoch was found until the next spring when his body floated up in the Detroit River, some distance downstream, in Canada. He had been dead for months. He had been shot in the head, and his body was tied and weighted down with a heavy pump chain. Unbelievably, the Canadian authorities simply pulled Knoch's body from the river and without so much as an inquest or any effort to identify him, they buried him. Later, relatives in Springwells saw a newspaper story of a body being found downriver, and notified the Knoch family. They went to Canada, exhumed the body, identified it as Charles Knoch, and took him home to bury. Wayne County authorities held an inquest, and held that Charles Knoch was murdered and came to his death by persons unknown.

The women of Springwells whispered among themselves how Mrs. Christine Knoch showed so little emotion after losing her husband and now her son in such tragic ways. It was up to local gossip to offer speculation on who may be responsible for Charles' death. Law enforcement officials believed it to be a robbery-murder, but had no suspects and no witnesses. There were theories put forth that Charles was robbed and killed by a disgruntled itinerant worker, because the chain around Charles' chest was one that was from the Knoch farm.

The Knoch Family was curiously silent on the whole matter, and the family closed ranks. They were very private and very stoic when they were in public. They had few associates. As a rule, they rarely socialized with neighbors or friends, preferring to keep their business to themselves. Mrs. Knoch in particular was very protective of her sons and daughters. It was said that although the Knoch men ran the business, Mrs. Knoch ruled the family, and her word was law in the Knoch household.

With the father Christian dead and the oldest son Charles dead, Frank Knoch became the head of the family business. Frank and the late Charles had invested in property outside the Knoch farm along Dix. Mrs. Knoch was against this from the start but the boys forged on with their business plans. Frank married a local Catholic girl, and his mother was not fond of her. Frank had also moved out of the family home with his new wife to the large tract of land in Springwells at what is now Riverside and Ferney Streets. Frank's land backed up to the narrow waterway called Baby Creek, which emptied into the Rouge at the western edge of his property. Frank and his wife had two children, and they were prosperous, growing onions and flowers which sold quickly at the markets in Detroit.

Two younger Knoch brothers remained at home. Gus was the third son and Herman was the fourth. Herman had a history of mental problems, was prone to unexplained angry outbursts and was manic at times. Gus and this brother were close. Gus seemed to be able to control Herman when no one else could. Frank controlled the family business, and Gus and Herman were basically the support staff.

    The bad luck that seemed to loom over the Knochs couldn't get any worse than it did in 1885. In the dead of night, a fire broke out in Frank's cabin. Some inebriated men leaving a pub on Fort Street came out at closing time and and saw the fire's glow and smoke in the sky. By the time they could give out the alarm to surrounding farmers, the cabin was completely engulfed. A bucket brigade from Baby Creek was futile. Horrified neighbors were scooping up and throwing snow on the roaring flames. A desperate search among onlookers showed that Frank, his wife and two young sons were nowhere to be found. The heat was unbearable and a rescue of the family could not be attempted.

Shown is an illustration of the fire in the cabin inhabited by Frank Knoch and his family. The home was utterly destroyed and the bodies were found later.

An illustration of Frank and Susan Knoch, derived from a newspaper sketch.

The Knoch family was alerted and ran to the scene. As with the onlookers, they only stood by helplessly as the cabin was consumed by the fire.

At daylight, gawkers from miles around came to the site. Sobbing quietly, ladies in their long dresses and winter wraps stood about and shook their heads. The smoldering remains of the farm cabin lay black and still. The barn and stable were untouched, and the Knochs removed Frank's stock to their own stable to care for the terrified animals.

Detroit Police and Wayne County Sheriff George Stellwagen's men were anxious to explore and sift through the cabin's debris when it cooled down.

Frank Knoch, his wife and two small sons were dead. Law enforcement wanted to be sure it was the accident it seemed to be.

Soon, the police no longer believed that the Knoch family had the worst bad luck on record. The fire was not an accident.

Frank's family's remains were found, what little charred flesh and bone was left. Frank and his wife had bullets in their brains. The skulls of the baby and toddler may have been crushed prior to the fire. It appeared that their bodies may have been chopped up. The blackened remains were placed in the Knoch's barn for examination by Wayne County morgue doctors.

Investigators found a burned up hatchet near the bodies of the babies. Gus Knoch and his brother Herman were also sifting through the remains. What were they looking for? They barely spoke to onlookers, even to questions directed to them by acquaintances. Gus spoke to a newspaper reporter that he thought his family was in the news too much and the publicity ought to stop.

While the inquest was going on and while the people were being questioned as to who may have seen the Frank Knoch family before the night of the fire, Gus was taking charge of the family business. Gus got along well with his mother. They were able to do the bookkeeping for the business in relative harmony and agreement. Again, the Knoch family was stoic and stone-faced in public. At the hearings, Gus testified that Frank's business was not going well and that Frank had bills he couldn't pay. This was in contrast to what Frank's neighbors and business associates claimed. Gus also testified that he knew Frank had a gun of the same caliber that was suspected to be the murder weapon. But Gus also owned the same kind of gun.

Naturally, a murder-suicide scenario had crossed the minds of the police. Had Frank Knoch killed his children, his wife and then set the fire and killed himself? The Knoch family was questioned. The family of Frank's wife, the Wittmans, also were questioned. They were emotional during questioning and could barely contain their sorrow and fury at what had happened.

Folks in the surrounding Springwells community had their own ideas about what happened. They felt that Gus and his brother Herman had killed Frank and his whole family to gain control of the growing Knoch empire. In this traditional German family, only a male heir could inherit the reins of the family business. People gossiped. Since Gus needed to get rid of Frank, they speculated, he also would need to get rid of Frank's two sons, who would inherit in their father's place. The scenario that wagging tongues had created grew into a story that most people agreed upon. The taverns were full of men talking about it. On the roads, sitting in the parked carriages were the womenfolk. They were being served beer by scurrying wait staff. Openly talking about the murders of Frank Knoch and his family, folks also talked about the "murders" of Christian and Charles Knoch.

Details of these previous deaths in the Knoch family were re-hashed among the people in the Springwells community. The chain that had held Charles Knoch's body underwater for six months had come from the well on the Knoch property, this was known. Christian Knoch's head wound: Kicked by a horse or beaten by his own greedy sons? When Christian lingered for a day in his bed before succumbing, his wife said he told her that the horse kicked him. A doctor thought that his head wound was so severe that he would never have regained consciousness and never been able to speak. And wasn't it Christian's cold-hearted wife who barely shed a tear over her husband or her son's death?

The theory that it was "bad luck" that the Knoch family suffered through was, for all intents and purposes, completely abandoned by the populace.

The community now had Gus Knoch and his weak-minded, temperamental brother Herman firmly in their sights. The two were depicted as being serial killers who preyed on their own family. And what better motivation did Gus and his brother have than inheriting money, property and a thriving business? People had wondered if the Wittmans would also inherit some of Frank's property, but Mrs. Knoch produced papers showing that Frank and Susan had owed her money, which would have to be paid before any inheriting is done. And the amount was large enough to cover most of what Frank owned.

All of this activity was not unnoticed by law enforcement officials.

The funeral of the family of four passed the still-smoldering remains of Frank Knoch's home. While the Wittmans wailed and sometimes drowned out the preacher during services, the Knoch family barely whimpered. Frank's sisters openly grieved, but Mrs. Knoch, Gus and Herman never lost their composure.

Illustration of little George and Frank, Jr., the two young sons of Frank Knoch

Later, the remains were dug up and more doctors examined them, right on the grounds of Woodmere cemetery, within sight of Frank's property. The prosecutor wanted an exact accounting of the remains; how much of each victim had been recovered, and exactly the wounds that could be discerned. Frank and Susan Knoch were shot in the head, definitely one small child's skull was crushed by a blow, and the recovered remains of the other child was so miniscule that it could not accurately be determined if this child was beaten to death. In one coffin, in one grave, the Frank Knoch family was again laid to rest.

Three weeks later, Mrs. Christine Knoch was dying. Her

health had been fragile of late and she took a turn for the worse and was bed-bound. Her doctor did not think she would live long. She was weak and sickly, and had pneumonia. A police officer of German descent, Joseph Burger, came to visit her and conversed with her in German rather candidly. This was one day before she passed away. Mrs. Knoch was angry about the past events in the family, she was angry at outsiders who questioned her sons, she was furious because she felt that the Wittmans had practically moved in with Frank and were taking over his business. She said Frank was too weak to stand up to it. She mentioned that he owed her money, said she had still expected to be paid.

Mrs. Christine Knoch, widowed and aged 61, died in January 1886, three weeks after the Frank Knoch family was wiped out.

If the gossip was any indication, the local populace was ready to lynch Gus and Herman. When a Dr. Owen declared that Mrs. Knoch was killed in her bed by savage blows to the head, angry mobs formed in the meeting halls and taverns along Dix and Fort streets. Rumor was that Gus and Herman Knoch would be dragged out and hanged from a tree in Woodmere Cemetery so that when Mrs. Knoch's funeral cortege passed by, all would see that justice had been served.

A month earlier in another sensational murder case, a huge mob rioted at the courthouse in Detroit. It was a case of a man who had stabbed and killed his fiancée. That angry crowd ripped the door off of an elevator that the man in custody was being transported in. They wanted the prisoner handed over to be beaten and lynched. They overran the police officers protecting the prisoner and every precinct in Detroit had to send men to the courthouse. The mob stampeded up the stairs to the courtroom on the third floor, and a hundred people were nearly crushed and some were injured. Sheriff Stellwagen was determined to prevent an incident such as that. He knew that it was his duty to do so.

Stellwagen was tired of waiting for word from the Prosecutor to arrest Gus and Herman. The peoples' fury was rising to an alarming level. He went to the Knoch household and arrested them. Based on Stellwagen's experience as a lawman, he knew that it was more of a "protective custody" arrest than a criminal arrest. He secreted the two Knoch brothers in a carriage and transported them to the county jail in Detroit before anyone got wind of it.

Stellwagen, by his prompt actions, probably saved their lives.

Christina Knoch was buried. At the service, her daughters wept. They were comforted by a few older German ladies who felt that in this time of need, the Knoch family needed to receive compassion more than retribution.

When the Wayne County Prosecutor had several other medical experts examine Mrs. Knoch's body, they concluded she had died of natural causes, namely pneumonia. Her attending physician testified that Mrs. Knoch suffered from severe pneumonia before her death, and that he had forewarned the family that she was not going to recover. Dr. Owen who made the mistake then reluctantly signed off on his earlier findings. It was ruled that the fracture to Mrs. Knoch's skull was caused by this same doctor when he when he examined the brain at the initial autopsy. The shameful mistake of declaring Mrs. Knoch's natural death to be a murder was talked about in the doctor's peer circles for a long time to come.

For lack of evidence, Gus and Herman were freed.

There were no more murders in the Knoch family. Gus and Herman remained on the original Christian Knoch farmstead. Frank's property was sold off. Herman continued to have mental problems, mainly it was his temper and his threats to do violence that undermined his ability to have a normal life. Gus had Herman permanently committed to an asylum in Pontiac in 1892. He died in 1911 from "exhaustion."

Gus Knoch was now at the helm of the Knoch family business, and he became a very wealthy man. He married and had several children who also went into the flower business. Gus built a sumptuous mansion, flower shop, greenhouse and conservatory on Fort Street near Woodmere Cemetery and his business took off. The Knochs had a winter place in Florida. They were known to circulate in the high society of the day with millionaires and captains of industry.

It could be said that Gus married a gal just like dear old mom, for Mrs. Minnie Knoch was a hard worker and a force to be reckoned with when it came to business decisions. When her children were small they worked in the greenhouse. Long hours and unrelenting plantings and cultivating were the rule of the household.

All seemed to be well, and the Knoch family was thriving and prosperous, but the ominous "bad luck" cloud descended again. One day Gus and wife Minnie were having a heated argument about money. She was angry about Gus' spending and he was worried the family finances couldn't cover their lifestyle. She had ideas for the family finances, to keep things on an even keel, but he thought that the situation was not good. Whatever else transpired between the couple, it was obvious that Gus was convinced that the business was going to go downhill and fail.

He hanged himself that day in 1917 in the beautiful home he had built. Gus Knoch was 52 years old.

The "Knoch Family Tragedies" seemed to know no bounds.

Minnie Knoch continued in the florist business, as did her

children and several of her grandchildren. The grandchildren were expected to work when they came to visit Grandma. No one was allowed to loiter or play while there were plants to pot and ship, deliveries to be made, and supplies to be purchased and paid for. One of Gus and Minnie's granddaughters Muriel Lobb went into the family business and with her husband opened a flower shop in Lincoln Park. Their granddaughter runs the shop at the present time, but does not want to continue this work into another generation. Perhaps the Knoch family's flower business is one of the oldest and continuing businesses in Michigan, running from the 1850s into the 21st century. Probably this generation will be its final link.

The events of the murders and suspicious deaths are long in the past. Christian Knoch's property is now a Detroit junkyard and scrap metal yard, walled off and inaccessible. It appears to be a veritable brownfield, with tall weeds and small trees overrunning some of it. West of this property is Holy Cross Cemetery, and across the street is Woodmere Cemetery in which so many of the late Knoch family members repose.

Frank Knoch's property became a Dearborn residential neighborhood across from the Ford Rouge Steel Plant and other small industrial plants. Where Baby Creek passed through Frank's property is now just a dry ditch, the creek having been filled in decades ago. Where it gently emptied its fresh spring water into the Rouge, among willow trees and wetland grasses is changed forever. Now the creek and river have been cut to make a canal passable for large ships. A small island was formed by this cut, Fordson Island. Interestingly enough, where Frank's house stood is a large empty lot or two, even to this day. No house has ever been built on that particular plot of land. Old timers in the neighborhood say there never was a house built there in their memory. There were houses and flats lined up in a row all along that street, except for the spot where the cabin of Frank Knoch burned down in 1885.

The vast farmland and meadows in Dearborn's South End that sprang up from woods, streams and sand ridges are long gone. Part of Springwells was annexed to Detroit, the other part became Dearborn. The community's property of the 1850s was purchased by Ford and then graded, compressed and paved over. The streams and creeks were either buried in pipes or filled in, wiped out by industrial plows and powerful earthmovers. Trees were cut and hauled off, farm houses knocked down and fences and walls built. The Rouge River was cut, channeled, and dredged. Its waters were warmed and churned, its aquatic life almost obliterated by the steel plant. The fresh air was dirtied by the pluming smokestacks. The factories, buildings and equipment seemingly had no end. The Ford Rouge Steel plant was a wonder in its time, taking in raw materials and producing finished automobiles. Thousands came for the jobs and the prosperity the plant offered the average man.

The land around the plant was subdivided, platted out for homes, apartments, hotels, bars, restaurants, doctor's offices and pharmacies. Remnants of Baby Creek and all her tributaries still exist in the serene pond in Woodmere Cemetery, and the swampy land in Patton Park. The Dix Avenue of the 19th century is nothing like it was. There isn't a single recognizable orchard, garden or any plot of land that hasn't been developed, and redeveloped over the past 150 years, except perhaps the cemeteries.

Where are those sprawling gardens and onion fields, the stables and barns and outhouses? What's become of the farmhouses and silos in Dearborn's south end? Large residential areas containing houses, apartments and hotels built during the booming automobile production years have been demolished and grassy lots now stand in their place. New construction has come to the area. No one remembers Baby Creek, Campbell Creek, or Roulo Creek. Early family names survive in the area's street names:

Miller, Roulo, Dix, Schaefer, Lonyo. Certainly lost is the North Dearborn Road. Smokestacks and the mills continuously operate and probably will for a long time to come.

Pictured is Gus Knoch's daughter-in-law Olive holding baby Muriel Knoch about 1919 in front of the store.

Most of Abel's family including Charles Johnesse moved to Oregon in the years following the war. Here pictured is Shaw's youngest brother James with his children and grandchildren about 1915.

CHAPTER 2

Abel Shaw and The Sharpshooters

bel Shaw was born in Detroit in 1843. His mother Rose Rivard was from one of the earliest families to settle in Detroit. The Rivard family had extensive land holdings on the east side of Detroit and Grosse Pointe. Shaw's father, Abel William Shaw was born in Massachusetts in 1815, and married Rose in Detroit in 1841. From this union were born three sons: Abel, Edmund and James.

By 1854, both parents had died, and Mr. and Mrs. Oliver Bellair took the boys in along with their own six children. Oliver Bellair had been appointed the boys' guardian and he was able to manage the boys' inheritance for their continuing support.

Oliver Bellair came from a distinguished French Detroit family also, and was related to the Rivards. It seemed natural that a wealthy, prominent businessman like Bellair to take the Shaw boys in. The three orphaned boys lived with the Bellairs and their children in Detroit. When the Civil War broke out, Abel Shaw was 17 years old and a blacksmith's apprentice. Brother Edmund was 15, while youngest brother James was 11.

In late 1862, Michigan needed to provide more than 4,000 men for the war effort. In Jackson, Michigan, Charles DeLand, a politically connected newspaper publisher and abolitionist raised the First Michigan Sharpshooters. In Detroit, Oliver Bellair was an army recruiter during the war and took his job seriously. He recruited his own son Oliver, along with his wards Abel and Edmund Shaw. All three entered into the service in the First Michigan Sharpshooters Regiment. Young men during these times were eager to serve, and the Bellair boy, along with his younger Shaw cousins was no different. Also recruited at the same time into this regiment was Charles Johnesse, who was likely an in-law to the Bellairs and a cousin to the Shaws.

The men of the First Michigan Sharpshooters arrived for duty at the Detroit Arsenal in Dearborn in the spring of 1863. They never dreamed they would be stationed there for months.

At Dearbornville, in the spring of 1863, the Civil War was well underway and reports of battles and casualties were big news in the town.

Shown is an illustration of the horrible tragedy in which Shaw lost his life. The report of the gun would have brought everyone running. Local doctors including Dr. Edward Sparrow Snow tended to Shaw but could not save him.

After a many long weeks of being stationed at Dearbornville, the First Michigan Sharpshooters were still being trained and disciplined as soldiers. The rules at the Dearbornville Arsenal were strict: Reveille was at 7 a.m. and lights out at 9 p.m. Orders were drafted forbidding the soldiers to allow civilians in camp without permission. Lots of civilians came to the camp to play cards and gamble, as did other "hucksters" looking to divide the soldiers from their pay. Orders were also drafted to make the men more responsible not only for the cleanliness but also the whereabouts of their uniforms. It was suspected that citizens were walking off with coats and jackets.

The Officers in charge kept the recruits drilling and doing guard duty four hours per day to fight the recruits' boredom and to keep them physically active and healthy. The men in charge hoped to also lessen the temptations of the soldiers to overstay their leaves. But the soldiers were aching for some action, and the inhabitants of the little village of Dearbornville complained about the soldiers getting drunk and disorderly, dating the girls in town and passing bad bank notes in the village businesses.

The guardhouse, which was located at what is now the northwest corner of Monroe and Garrison, was frequently inhabited by men doing time for inappropriate behavior. One troublemaker got five days on bread and water and then five days of solitary confinement for gross misconduct and insubordination. The majority of soldiers had good service records, but there were those who got into trouble time and time again.

There was no denying it; after many long weeks stationed at the Arsenal, the First Michigan Sharpshooters were aching for their marching orders.

The guard duty detail at the arsenal was not so much to guard against someone breaking in to steal guns and ammunition, or to sabotage the Union Army's war efforts. The soldiers who were on this detail were not even allowed to carry loaded guns. Guard duty was mainly to keep the men from being idle and to keep the soldiers stationed within from sneaking out. And sneak out they did. Whether it was in the dark of night or with forged passes, the guys found ways to get out to socialize and drink.

Often pranksters targeted someone on guard duty. They would surreptitiously fill the weapon with sand or stop up the tubes to make the gun unserviceable. This of course would lead to punishment if the soldier did not discover it or could not clean it out without a superior officer finding out.

When being relieved of the guard duty detail, the officers would face each other and snap the locks on their weapons. Since all weapons were unloaded, this resulted in a loud snap sound and the relieved soldier then could leave his post and goes his way. One of the ways that the guys had fun was for someone to sneak a charge into a soldiers' gun when he went on guard duty. When they were relieved, they snapped the gun, it went off, and the startled soldier's reaction was always good for a laugh for the men. The charge would make a very loud report and was relatively harmless as there was no ball loaded.

In early May, 1863, Private Abel Shaw was being relieved of his guard duty detail and did not know that he was to become the butt of a prank. Some jokester had tampered with Shaw's weapon and had loaded it. When Shaw was relieved, several men who were in on the fun came by. Shaw stood with his weapon, with the muzzle under his arm, chatting with some other men. But Shaw hadn't snapped his lock, so Private Charles Johnesse snuck up behind him and snapped it with his foot. Shaw's gun went off, but to everyone's horror they realized that the jokester had also loaded a ball into it. The ball blasted mercilessly through Shaw's upper arm and shoulder. The young soldier dropped. The wound was grave and Shaw bled profusely. He was near death when the camp surgeons tended to him and deliberated on a course of action to try to save the 20-year-old's life.

The Detroit Free Press reported this incident as "A Sad Accident at Dearborn" and stated that the soldier's arm had to be amputated and that there was no hope for recovery.

Army surgeons had actually not amputated the whole arm, but had re-sectioned some of the damaged areas and were in the hope of giving Shaw some semblance of a working limb should he recover.

E.J. Buckbee, Adjutant, by order of Colonel Charles DeLand, wrote in his orders of the day on May 11, 1863:

"It is with the deepest regret that the Colonel has heard that Private Abel W. Shaw has been seriously if not mortally wounded today, by gross carelessness in the use of firearms while doing guard duty. It has been the practice of some wicked and vicious men to load the guns used by the Guard…As expected, this piece of willful mischief has finally by the aid of a thoughtless and wayward boy culminated in the sad disaster which may result yet in the death of one of the best and most reliable men of the Regiment. It can result in nothing less than crippling and maiming him for life. However much we may be inclined to censure the boy Johnesse, he is guiltless compared with the wretch who had converted the gun into an infernal machine to deal death and misfortune upon an innocent man. While it is my duty to order Charles Johnesse under arrest, it is my deepest regret that I cannot also punish the more guilty party. Let this sad casualty be a lesson to all not to repeat the carelessness of which today we have had so severe a lesson."

Shaw held on to dear life for about a month, but died June 5, 1863 in Dearborn. He was the regiment's first casualty to firearms. The tally of triumphs and losses of the First Michigan Sharpshooters' journeys during the Civil War began with the death of Private Abel Shaw at the Dearbornville Arsenal. The rest is history.

A view outside the Arsenal Gates in Dearbornville about 1860.

This is a photograph of the original Miller cabin that Denison Miller built when he arrived in the USA. When a better home was built nearer to Michigan Avenue, Denison Miller used this cabin as an outbuilding and stable over the years. The Miller home stood in the parking area at the rear of Wonderland Music Store, Michigan Avenue east of Schaefer.

CHAPTER 3

Mrs. Miller Let The Cat Out

n a cold November night in 1871, Mr. and Mrs. Denison Miller slept peacefully in their small farm home on the Chicago Road. The Miller's home was on land they purchased when they settled in Michigan thirty five years earlier.

The couple had known a good life in Greenfield Township, Michigan. They raised their children here and the Miller clan had then spread out and settled on land all the way from Schaefer Road to beyond Miller Road.

The Chicago Road, now known as Michigan Avenue, was a main thoroughfare. A dirt road only two lanes wide, it had a toll booth in the vicinity of Wyoming St., and one near what is now Southfield Rd. It carried a lot of traffic to and from Detroit. In the early morning hours, farmers from the outlying areas of Detroit travelled inbound to sell their produce and stock. In the afternoons, folks depended on the Chicago Road to get to local farms and business places.

The Millers were a contented married couple. They had accumulated enough wealth to live on in their golden years. Although only in their late 50s, they were considered elderly at the time.

Their neighbors across the street, the Schaefers, ran the Six Mile House and Tavern, complete with a stable and blacksmith shop. To the west were the Maples, Chases and Woodworths, and to the east were the Haggertys, Campbells, and Reuters.

The Millers lived frugally. The log cabin they had occupied when first coming to the Dearborn area was still standing near their present farmhouse. They had a small orchard, a garden, and their children and grandchildren nearby. Life for the Millers was good.

On this November night in 1871 however, all that changed.

Mrs. Miller awoke just after midnight when she heard an odd sound outside under the bedroom window sill. A few minutes later, the cat in the kitchen mewed loudly. Not wanting to disturb her husband Denison, Jane Miller rose quickly and quietly and went to attend to the cat. She unbolted the back door, cracked it just enough and the cat ran out. To her utter shock, an intruder forced the door open wider and moved quickly into the kitchen. Mrs. Miller could not see the man clearly. He stepped up to her menacingly and she screamed. The man warned to her keep quiet, but she ran to her bedroom yelling, "Murder!"

Instantly Denison Miller was out of bed and grappling with the intruder. The men tumbled around the room knocking over furniture. Mrs. Miller joined in the fracas. Suddenly there was a gasp... and both men stood still for an instant. Then Mr. Miller shrank down and collapsed to the floor. Mrs. Miller embraced him. She saw that the intruder was still gripping a knife buried in her husband's chest. "Don't murder him!" she sobbed. She also grasped the knife blade as the intruder pulled it free. Later she would realize that her palm had been cut. The man then left as quickly as he came. He took nothing and said nothing more.

The Miller's nephew who had been staying in the house ran into the room seconds later and then out the door in pursuit of the stranger. He did not see anyone in the moonlit night, could not find any trial to follow. The night was cold and still.

They raised a hue and cry to the neighbors and the sheriff was summoned. Lamps were lit in windows all over that part of town. People dressed for the cold and ventured outside. The word spread quickly.

Mr. Miller had died instantly on his bedroom floor, having

been stabbed once, straight through the heart.

In the ensuing days there was a great uproar in the Miller home and the environs. No one could understand why someone would have committed a cold-blooded murder such as this. What kind of burglar was this? Burglars are usually content to sneak into a home. They try to avoid contact with the inhabitants. This kind of burglary was a dangerous business. An intruder could be shot by an armed occupant of the home.

Just beyond the parlor, and its door on a line with the front door, is the kitchen, a large old fashioned room, with a great cook stove in the center. In this room were gathered a score or more of farmers, some feeling awed by the presence of death in the bed-room beyond, others indignant and anxious to revenge the murder. News of the affair had traveled miles away, and the honest farmers had turned out to sympathize with the widow and offer their services to help hunt down the villain who made her thus.

Quote in the paper.

The large, grieving Miller family could offer no answers to law enforcement, nor offer a name of a suspect who would have had a motive to kill the likable Denison Miller. Wasn't he a man who kept to his own business? Wasn't he the man who donated property to the township for a school? At first the family objected to a post-mortem examination of Mr. Miller's body, as they wanted to follow the local tradition of laying the body out in the home and having a funeral within a day or two.

However, a valuable clue in this murder investigation lay in determining the type of murder weapon used. This could only be accomplished by a close and careful look at the deadly wound. The family did consent to the exam which was performed on the premises. Several doctors were called in and, by examining Miller's heart, they concurred that the murder weapon had been a dagger.

Neighbors from all around the Greenfield, Springwells, and Dearborn Townships were in attendance at the Miller home for the funeral service and in the sad days that followed. The Maples, Chovins, Theisens, Klosens, and many others offered up their sentiments. The feeling among the family and friends was that this crime would probably never be solved. Mrs. Miller could not identify anyone as the murderer. She never saw him clearly and believed he had a dark cloth masking his face.

Sheriff's deputies went over the scene of the crime and found drops of blood on the ground where the murderer made his successful escape. They found that he had left the carriage gate propped open so that he could dash out into the darkness of that cold November night unimpeded. The murder weapon was not found.

Denison Miller, age 55, was buried in the Scotch Settlement Cemetery (Evergreen Cemetery) on Warren near Southfield Road.

For law enforcement, the problem with solving the murder of Denison Miller was that the killer seemed to have no clear motive. This man seemed to have been casing the Miller home. If burglary was his intent, he should have waited for Mrs. Miller to let the cat out and go back to bed.

Burglary and robbery are different crimes. Both involve stealing, but robbery is stealing something by the use of force or a threat of force. If he planned to rob the Millers by assaulting the couple and threatening them unless they cooperated, then the only thing the killer did right was use the element of surprise. He failed to gain control of the couple's movements. When he burst in, he lost control of Mrs. Miller as she dashed for the bedroom and in the chaos that ensued, Mr. Miller was stabbed. Nothing was stolen from the home.

Was the killer's intent to rob, or was it his intent to kill someone and make it seem like a robbery gone wrong?

There was the strong possibility that the man who murdered Denison Miller had planned to commit murder. His motive seemed to be to cause a confrontation, and then experience the thrill of the kill.

The thought of a person running loose in the neighborhood who kills for fun struck terror into the hearts of the citizens. A fiend such as this cannot be reasoned with because he enjoys the thrill and the danger he seeks. He will follow his urges to strike out. If he gets away with his crime, he may do it again. If he chooses a victim, then that person is surely marked for death. Is this what happened to poor Mr. Miller?

The people were nervous, especially those who lived up and down the Chicago Road in this township that would someday be Dearborn. People talked about the murder in church and on street corners and in taverns. Recounting other nighttime burglaries that had taken place, people began buying guns. Instead of being content with small-caliber hunting rifles, farmers began purchasing shotguns and revolvers, man-killers, to protect themselves. They were convinced, as the police in Detroit and the Wayne County Sheriffs were also, that this may not just be the work of a bold burglar.

Many people were questioned by the authorities. Most folks who were awake that night were innkeepers and toll booth keepers. One man who lived south of the Millers became the focus of the police. His name was Dennis Carroll, and he had the unfortunate luck of having been on the Chicago Road around the time of the murder. Carroll was with his young nephew, and was going home after a day's labor. He stopped in at two taverns and his team of horses wandered off at some point and turned up at the toll booth at Wyoming St. The young nephew came after them and led them away. The bartenders and the toll booth operator all readily identified Carroll as being the man who was out late that night, but all said that he was very inebriated. It was intimated that Carroll could barely walk much less run to escape the murder scene. Dennis Carroll was in the spotlight for several days until his alibi was established and it was airtight: He was in one of the taverns at precisely the time Miller was killed and for a length of time afterward. Mrs. Miller looked at Carroll, and, under oath, testified that she could not say whether he was the man who killed her husband. Carroll was cleared. The case went cold.

Life in the Township of Greenfield went on. Farmers still had their chores to tend to, animals still needed to be fed and watched over. Housewives cooked and cleaned, and dipped into their winter's rations of food they'd put up. Apples and potatoes were drawn up from the storage bins. The Christmas holidays came and went. Folks were careful about their nighttime routines, and kept a wary eye on strangers in town. No other murders or burglaries occurred in the area.

In the spring of 1872 someone had maliciously placed obstructions on the railroad tracks at the approach where the MCRR tracks cross the Rouge River in Dearborn Township. The passenger train was able to stop and only sustained minimal damage, and luckily no passengers were hurt. This was not the work of merry pranksters or mischievous boys…this person intended for the train and passenger cars to be thrown off the tracks and plunge into the Rouge. A young man was arrested for the act, and charged. When questioned by law enforcement, he admitted what he had done. When the officers asked the young man what he could possibly have gained by hurting hundreds of people he didn't even know, the man said that he merely did it to see what it would be like.

That young man was William Smith, a farmhand on the Maples farm, next door to Denison Miller's farm.

After Smith's family posted bond, Smith wasted no time in getting into trouble again. This time he walked to Ecorse and burned down a barn. Apprehended yet again, he sat in the lockup bragging to his cellmate about how he likes to do things for the thrill of it, even murdering the old man at the Miller place.

The sheriff immediately questioned Smith about Miller's death. The coolness and matter-of-fact manner that Smith portrayed was frightening. He admitted killing Miller. He bragged about how he did it and how he was successful in his getaway. The sheriff had a hard time believing that Smith, who was barely 17 when he killed Miller could show no remorse or emotion of any kind over it.

William Smith offered up details about his movements the night Denison Miller was killed. Smith shared a bedroom with the Maples' son who was about Smith's age. When the Maples boy had fallen asleep, Smith chloroformed him to ensure that he stayed asleep. He then crept out of the house through the bedroom window, down onto a shed roof and then jumped to the ground. He propped up a ladder against his bedroom window. With his dagger in his pocket, he made his way stealthily over to the Millers' and peered in their bedroom window as they slept. He intended to find a way to get into the house. When he saw Mrs. Miller get up to let the cat out, Smith could hardly believe his good luck. He hurried to the kitchen door and burst in when she unbolted it.

As soon as Smith got away and arrived back at the Maples' home, he crept into his room and let the ladder down to the ground with a rope. He got back into bed and waited for the news of the awful deed to spread. The next morning, Smith said he went with the Maples family over to the Miller's house where several carriages were parked and dozens of people had gathered. A length of black crepe was tied to the door handle to indicated mourning within. Mrs. Miller was nearly frantic. She readily went over the details of the murder with the visitors; how she let the cat out and let evil in. Smith said that he viewed Miller's body, laid out in his bed, still in his bloody nightclothes.

While confessing, Smith told the sheriff that he gave the dagger to a peddler passing through the area. Then he bought the knife back from the peddler and paid the peddler to tell folks he had just sold a knife to Smith. However, no one came looking to Smith for the knife, so he then sold it to another young man. Smith was proud of his attention to detail. He was happy to admit how he had arranged to get his knife back into his own possession after the murder, and therefore be above suspicion, if anyone had questioned him. Smith had "practiced" with his dagger. He confessed that he had stabbed and killed a neighbor farmer's horse with it.

The prosecutor and other law enforcement officials were notified, and Smith's dagger was tracked down, having been passed through other hands during the months after Miller's murder. The doctors examined the dagger and concurred that it was similar to what they had concluded would likely be the murder weapon.

Miller's family and neighbors were astounded by Smith's arrest and confessions. Some said that he must have an "unsound mind," or "disordered brain," and that Denison Miller surely died at the hands of a madman. Everyone knew that Smith had no reason to set his sights on Miller. The Maples were horrified when they thought how their son had been sharing a room with Smith.

William Smith's mother pleaded her son's case to the sheriff. She said that Smith had sustained a terrible head injury when he was small, and took a long time to recover from it. She said he was never quite right after that. Smith's father said that when Smith was 12 years old, he dug out a hole underneath their house and insisted on sleeping there instead of in his own bed. Smith ran away from home and no one heard anything from him until he inexplicably returned home at age 14. Becoming a farm hand was the most they could hope for their son. No one in his family thought Smith was a homicidal maniac. No one thought that he could commit murder. Smith's family felt that his strange behavior over the years had to at least show that he was not of sound mind. Smith, though, did not consider himself to be "crazy."

Several doctors who interviewed and examined Smith said he was sane and fit to be charged.

Smith pleaded not guilty. His defense attorneys planned for the "not guilty by reason of insanity" defense.

While awaiting trial, Smith told the sheriff that he was guilty, but he wanted "to make them prove it." Smith said that he would rather be locked up than be free because he didn't want to have to work his whole life.

Smith got his wish and was found guilty and sentenced to life in prison.

Pictured is Joseph Schaefer's Six Mile House at the northeast corner of Michigan and Schaefer. Schaefer had a tavern, a blacksmith shop, a small grocery store, rooms to let, and a barn and stable. It was a meeting place for townspeople of Springwells where official notices of local interest were posted by the authorities. Behind the Schaefer House was a well-mown commons and picnic area that the Schaefer family maintained for Sunday picnics and baseball games.

One of the homes of Miller's many descendants was located at
Miller Road and Michigan Avenue.

Denison Miller's grandson Frank was just a baby when his grandfather was killed.

Here is a sketch of Mary Mehl made from a newspaper illustration

CHAPTER 4

Mary's Apple Tree

eventeen-year-old Mary Mehl walked breezily down Michigan Avenue in the evening hours of August 10, 1898. Observers recalled seeing her in a buoyant mood, brightly waving her handkerchief as she neared the westerly limits of the Village of Dearborn. Mary's disposition that night was a marked change from her mood of late; she had been seen many times in the previous few weeks walking alone through town, weeping quietly and avoiding encounters with anyone. But this evening, the girl seemed to be transformed. With her hair piled high and pinned up, she wore a neat, long skirt and high-collared blouse, and her cheeks had taken on a rosy bloom befitting a young lady in love.

At Papke's 10 mile house at the southeast corner of Michigan Avenue and Monroe, locals pose for this photograph about 1890. Mary Mehl's father Charles Mehl, employed in the brickyards at the time, is the rather diminutive, dirty-looking chap standing 6th from the right.

Mary Mehl was certainly in love.

Just that afternoon, she had found a chance to sneak away from all the chores she had been hired to take on by Ted Neuendorf and his wife, Sophia. Mary found two of the Neuendorfs' nieces and sent them to the Dearborn train station in town. In their possession the giggling girls had a note from Mary for the man she was crazy in love with, Will Parrish. The little girls had delivered notes between the two young people before. But Mary seemed extra anxious to get this note to Will. She wasn't sure she could sneak away or make excuses to go into town to see Will herself. The Michigan Central Railroad's flag station where Will worked was at Mason Street and the tracks, not too far from the Neuendorfs'. A correspondence was necessary because, as Mary explained to her couriers, she needed to know if Will would meet her tonight in their secret place. The girls were dispatched and Mary was waiting for them when they returned.

This night, of all nights, was important, maybe the most important night of Mary's life. Tonight she would know when she and Will would be married. And then they would go to the Dearborn Village Cake-Walk and Dance at Village Hall and announce it to everyone. When the little girls returned with a note from Will saying simply, "Yes," Mary was elated. She told the girls that by the next day they would hear news that she was engaged.

That night, the dance in Dearborn carried on as expected with live music, good food and a large crowd. The lights were burning in Village Hall on Monroe Street until well past 10 p.m. Outside the dance hall, William Ross and his cousin Lytle had been drinking and jostling each other and laughing. In the dark, Lytle tripped and toppled over a shadowy figure on the lawn, then turned and apologized to what looked like a drunken man reclining in the grass. The man sat up, but said nothing. Eventually the Ross cousins staggered away, enjoying the summer night, but they looked over, many times, at the mysterious man still reclining in the grass. The inebriated cousins headed for their homes and thought nothing more of it.

Neither Mary nor Will showed up at the Cake-Walk and Dance.

The next morning, Mrs. Neuendorf went to Mary's room to wake her for the start of her chores. The girl often snuck out at night, and no one in the house knew what time she snuck back in. Mary was not the most reliable employee, and the Neuendorfs knew that when they took Mary in. Mary had been fired from other domestic servant jobs in the Village because she frequently disregarded her chores.   Mrs. Neuendorf did not interfere with Mary's surreptitious comings and goings in the evenings when her chores were finished. But on this morning, when Mary failed to report, her employer went to check on her. Finding Mary's room neat and her bed not slept in, Mrs. Neuendorf was puzzled. Soon though, word had spread throughout the Village of Dearborn: Mary Mehl's body had been found at dawn in an overgrown apple orchard just outside of town. Her throat had been cut from ear to ear.

In the days that followed, no one in the Village of Dearborn could talk about anything else. Justice of the Peace Allan Shaw and Village Marshal Charles Forsythe were the first officials on the scene. Village resident Frank Greenwald told how he had taken his cow to graze in the old orchard and had found the body. He ran to Franz Bischoff's place, on the south side of Michigan Avenue at Haigh Street, the closest house to the orchard, and raised the alarm.

The group of onlookers turned into a large, gawking crowd. Mary's body lay face up beneath a large apple tree that had one broken branch jutting out straight and low to the ground. It was obvious to everyone present that Mary had come to this place to meet someone. The branch was perfect for sitting on, the bark worn smooth, and the grass scraped away, indicating that it was a private and well-used meeting place, unseen from the roadway.

Mary's body was lying straight, one of her arms slightly bent outward and one at her side. Her clothes were still neat, and her skirt, stockings and shoes as they should be. Mary's blouse was unbuttoned at the neck and not torn. It was slightly stained by the large amount of blood from the gash in her throat. The blood had seeped into the ground below her. A straight razor lay at her side. There was blood on the razor, but none on Mary's hands. She appeared to have some bruises on her face and mouth. Someone found a small glass vial near Mary's body, but this item was never recovered by the law enforcement officers.

DEARBORN'S TRAGEDY.

D. D. TOMPKINS, Who Said He Recognized the Razor.

THE OLD PUMP AND BARREL, WHERE THE MURDERER IS SUP- POSED TO HAVE WASHED HIS HANDS.

An illustration from the newspaper at the time, shows citizens posed around the barn where the killer cleaned up.

Everyone in town was coming to the orchard, and all anyone could talk of was who the killer could be. Was this someone Mary Mehl knew or some random fiend who crossed paths with her last night? Why would someone do this? How could someone do this?

Conspicuously absent in the orchard that morning was Will Parrish. When undertaker Louis Howe picked up the body and conveyed it to his place, the townspeople realized how little they actually knew about Mary's private life. Only a few knew she was in love with Will. No one had ever seen them together in public as a couple. No one ever saw the person she was meeting in the orchard. Mary herself had only referred to her mysterious beau as Willie or "My Will." When Mary had talked to her few friends of her upcoming marriage, she always said that his name would be a secret until they made their announcement.

WILLIAM PARISH

Young Joseph William "Will" Parrish testifying at the inquest as to his knowledge regarding Mary Mehl's murder. (from a newspaper illustration)

But many people did know that Will Parrish was Mary Mehl's foster brother. When Mary's mother, Minnie, died in 1892, apparently during childbirth, her father, Charles Mehl, had many children and could not care for them properly. Solomon and Jane Parrish took Mary in when she was 10 years old and their own son Will was 13.

In the 18 months before Mary's

murder, the family experienced the loss of Solomon Parrish, and soon afterward Jane Parrish died. This left 20-year-old Will and 17-year-old Mary to fend for themselves on meager inheritances. Mary immediately took a job as live-in domestic help. Will got a railroad job as a flag man and did extra jobs around town for the money.

The only time anyone in town saw Mary with Will after the deaths of his parents was when Mary visited him at the train station. All summer she slipped into the station whenever she could, and when she was seen leaving, she was always crying.

While officials Shaw and Forsythe continued to search the crime scene at the apple orchard, a coroner's inquest was set up by undertaker Howe to determine the cause and manner of death. No one was really sure whom to notify because Mary's widowed father had since remarried and moved to Big Rapids. Mary had an adult brother who worked at the Wagner brickyard, but Will Parrish was the first one they thought of to notify. And to question.

The officials found Will in his rented room where he was boarding with the barber Ulysses S. Cranson and his wife, Mary. When he was called upon, Will said that Mary's death was news to him. He said he had not seen her in many days and didn't know of anyone who would want to kill her. He gladly accompanied the officials to the apple orchard to look over the crime scene.

By this time, some of the men there had followed footprints to a fence behind the railroad tracks, leading southeast. On the fence was a bit of blood; shoe prints on the other side led to a barn that was no longer in use. At this barn was a working hand pump, where, the officials surmised, the killer must have washed up. The trail ended there.

From the orchard, Will Parrish went to Howe's undertaking

rooms to view and positively identify the body of his foster sister, Mary Mehl.

Mary's father came from Big Rapids to attend her funeral service, which was standing-room only. She was buried in Northview Cemetery. Elba Howe was appointed director of Mary's estate, handling all the arrangements and even paying for a headstone himself.

A coroner's inquest determined that Mary had met her end by the cut to her throat, severing her jugular vein and windpipe – murder at the hands of someone unknown. The Dearborn doctor in attendance and the coroner determined that Mary had not been sexually assaulted and that she was "a chaste girl" whose "maidenhood" was intact.

Will Parrish was questioned by Shaw and Forsythe. He explained that he had worked the day Mary was killed, and then he had walked around town for a little while, stopping into shops here and there. He said he did go to the Cake-Walk and Dance, but did not go inside. As he reclined in the grass, Lytle Ross had tripped over him. Will said he lay for quite some time and then went to the barbershop and walked home with the barber Cranson. Will denied passing notes to Mary, denied meeting her at the apple tree, denied that she came often to the train station, and denied she had ever left the station crying. In fact, Will Parrish was so convincing that he wasn't questioned further.

The straight razor identified as the murder weapon was displayed for all to see in the hope that someone would know to whom it belonged. A reward was offered. The oldest resident in town, in his 80s, was "Ol' Dan Tompkins," who said the razor had once belonged to him, but that he had "sharped it up" and given it away. He could only remember that he had given it to a woman.

Pictured is Charles Forsythe, who served as Town Marshal when Mary Mehl was murdered. He was a very tall man, intelligent and well liked in the Dearbornville community. Townspeople mused how Forsythe rarely wore shoes from May to November.

With all these open-ended and contradictory statements from the citizens, putting together a scenario of what had happened to Mary Mehl was working out to be quite a monumental task. Having never experienced an event such as a homicide, much less ever having taken charge of investigating a homicide, officials Shaw and Forsythe were bound to make mistakes.

Entering into the case a few days afterward was Wayne County Prosecutor Allan Frazer. He sent deputies to the little Village of Dearborn to question everyone again. These men and subsequent investigators sent by Frazer uncovered a lot of clues and additional leads as to the identity of Mary's killer. They speculated on one very plausible scenario: Since Mary had bruises on her face and mouth, the little vial that was missing from the scene of the murder may have held chloroform. Mary could have been forcibly restrained with a cloth saturated in chloroform and roughly held over her face to knock

Will Parrish poses with the Goodfellows charitable group about 1927. He is the slim man at the very top right in the dark suit. Mayor Clyde Ford is front and center. To the far right is the Fire Chief Ed Nowka and Police Chief Fred Faustman.

her out. She could have then been put down into the grass, her blouse loosened and then her throat slit. This could explain the lack of blood on Mary's clothing and hands.

Many people came forward to testify that Mary met someone at the apple tree regularly because she was seen walking to that area at least once a week, when she would disappear off Michigan Avenue and descend into the orchard. It probably wasn't a stranger who killed Mary, the officials surmised, because the killer knew to run to the abandoned barn and knew that it still had a working water pump.

More details about Mary's personal life came to light. Mary had been fired as a domestic servant by at least two other families in the five months since her foster mother died. At every interview,

Mary's former employers complained of her being careless in her work and distracted with the idea of being in love, getting married and having a home of her own. Mary often snuck away from her chores and went into town, to the train station, making up flimsy excuses to her employers.

Young children testified that Mary used them as go-betweens to pass notes to Will, and that he would write back. Once, a little girl testified, she peeked at one of Mary's notes, a reminder to Will to meet her at the usual place and usual time. Several of these children and Mary's few friends testified that the name of her boyfriend was "Will." Most of these young people said they knew this to be Will Parrish.

Prosecutor Frazer's attention turned to Will, and he immediately ordered Will arrested and brought to the Dearborn Village Town Hall office for questioning. Shaw and Forsythe didn't think there was enough evidence to bring him in – and ignored Frazer's telephone message. A special investigator from Frazer's office, John Troy, came by train to Dearborn from Detroit and escorted Will to the Village Hall . Frazer was not a well-liked man in the small towns outside Detroit, including Dearborn. He was known as a big-city, by-the-book lawman. Frazer closed down taverns for liquor violations because local law enforcement officials mostly looked the other way. Frazer exposed county justices who accepted bribes and were involved in other criminal affairs. He jailed thieves working for local boards of education. He was feared and hated by many law enforcement officers who thought he used his discretionary powers unfairly.

When Frazer's appointed man brought Will in, Shaw, Forsythe and other local officials felt that the prosecutor was grandstanding. The resentment had built up. The locals were not as cooperative or forthcoming as they could have been.

When Frazer publicly questioned Will, he brought up all the discrepancies between Will's previous statements and those made by other residents under oath. Will conceded that Mary Mehl had come to the train station, but she had not visited often, and certainly had never cried when she was with him. Will conceded that perhaps once he and Mary had exchanged a note, but it was a note asking him the address of an aunt who lived in Birmingham. Will couldn't remember if Mary had sent a note the day she was killed. He denied ever meeting her at the apple tree in the orchard. He didn't think Mary ever expressed anything other than an affectionate, sisterly love for him, but Will Parrish knew one thing: He was not in love with Mary. Will stated that he had, in fact, a serious girlfriend and that he was seen publicly courting this other girl.

Will could not name anyone who could provide him an alibi for about an hour in the early evening the night Mary was murdered. He admitted he was the man that Lytle Ross tripped over the night of the dance, but that event did not account for Will's whereabouts from the time he got off work until he was seen outside the dance hall. Will said that he would like to see the case resolved as soon as possible and the killer apprehended and punished.

During a break in the questioning, for which nearly half the town turned out to witness, the prosecutor was approached by a prominent villager, 68-year-old Nathaniel Ross. Ross said he saw Will in possession of that straight razor six months earlier, as he attended an auction of household goods at the Parrish house after Jane Parrish had died. Ross said he had seen the straight razor for sale in a box and had told Parrish that he should keep the razor for himself. Ross said that Parrish then picked up and pocketed the razor.

When Frazer resumed the questioning of Will Parrish, he asked about the straight razor. Will denied owning it or having any conversation with Nathaniel Ross at the auction.

Will was calm and cool in his testimony. He even walked through the crime scene all the way to the barn to satisfy the officials, who looked for any change in his demeanor, any sign of nervousness or guilt. Will showed none. Will didn't even show sorrow for the tragic loss of his foster sister, whom he presumably had some affection for.

Pictured is Mary Mehl's headstone at Northview Cemetery. The top of the stone has Mehl printed on it, nearly worn off. Elba Howe was the undertaker and was also Mary Mehl's guardian. After her death he handled what little property was in her estate. An auction was not necessary. Howe held a raffle to sell Mary's property and some lucky person in the town won the organ from her foster home.

When the questioning at the inquest concluded, the jurors, made up entirely of local men, concluded that Mary Mehl had been murdered by a person or persons unknown. Will Parrish, having become quite a famous man in town, was freed. The Wayne County sheriff's office said it would keep on investigating, at Frazer's urging, if there was adequate funding.

But in the end, no one was ever tried for the murder of young, love-struck Mary Mehl, whose simple goal in life was to have a husband, a home and a family.

Mary's murder in the hamlet of Dearborn was certainly a mystery, but a larger mystery remains: Why didn't Will Parrish ever go to trial – even after an examination of the victim's body by Wayne County doctors two months after the homicide showed that Mary Mehl was pregnant at the time of her death?

This view is Michigan Avenue looking east between Howard and Mason. Mary walked past here and then would leave the road just past artist Franz Bischoff's house to get to the orchard. Today this would be the parking lot area west of ACE Hardware.

Perhaps Frazer himself had some doubt about Parrish's guilt. Perhaps he felt he could not win the case without more evidence, mindful that an acquittal would prevent Parrish from ever being tried again. Perhaps he felt a jury would acquit Parrish no matter what the evidence, just to spite Frazer for his tavern-busting activities. Or perhaps the prosecutor did not want a lost case such as this to taint his own political future.

As time went on, crowds continued to gather at the apple orchard, stopping at Mary's special tree to see where she met her lover and dared to dream her fondest dreams. Folks came by the hundreds, pointing to the spot in the soil where the blood had been found, and speculating openly on the details of the horrible crime. Young girls posed there to have their pictures taken. Souvenir hunters stripped off branches and apples from Mary's tree. People even circulated stories that seeds from the apples could sprout into trees bearing fruit with red streaks, symbolizing the blood from the heinous murder.

It is not known if anyone ever planted the seeds of any of Mary's apples, or what, if anything, happened when they did. What is known is that two years after Mary's death, in 1900, Will Parrish married his "real" girlfriend, Bessie Martin. Sometime after 1930, Will left his family, and although he lived in Dearborn, he remained estranged and never met any of his grandchildren. He held several public officer positions in Dearborn over the years.

The grave of Will Parrish lies unmarked today at Northview Cemetery, not far from the headstone of Bessie and her parents, Albert and Mary Martin of Dearborn. Twenty feet away stands the solitary headstone of Mary Mehl, so worn you can barely read it at all.

The railroad depot in Dearbornville where Mary often snuck away
to spend time with Will Parrish.

Pictured is the Franz Bischoff residence and property. Bischoff, a well known ceramic artist and painter, is out front with his family. The orchard was planted about the time of the Civil War by the Haigh family. The trees were aged and overgrown with grass. It had become somewhat of a commons where the townspeople grazed their animals.

CHAPTER 5

The Fatal Ride Of Hannah McQuade

round the McQuade farm, a dozen men milled about outside. No one spoke much, the mood was somber, and most of the men were smoking and standing about in small groups. It was an early evening in the summer of 1905 and the neighbors and family members of the McQuades were gathered here from all over the Greenfield Township and Detroit area.

Inside the beautiful farm house, Mrs. Hannah McQuade was sobbing loudly and was inconsolable in her grief over the death of her youngest child, her namesake, 7 year old Hannah. The small, still body of the little girl was laid upon the couch in the parlor, wrapped in white cloth. The women who had gathered inside the home were talking in hushed tones. Hannah's two older sisters were staying close to their mother, who would not leave the dead child's side.

Law enforcement officers had been coming and going, viewing the child's wound and speaking with the sisters. Detroit police, Wayne County Sheriffs, and the prosecutor had all stopped by the home. Everyone was trying to put together an accurate account of what had happened to little Hannah McQuade only hours earlier.

The gunshot wound in Hannah's forehead was obvious. There was still blood on her older sisters' clothing. The neighbor who had carried Hannah's lifeless body home from Dexter Road near Grand River still had blood on his clothing. Hannah McQuade's older brothers had fetched home the surrey carriage she was riding in, and had put the old farm horse into the barn.

The only bright spot, as if there really could be one, was that the culprit who shot and killed 7 year old Hannah had been arrested and was locked up. The shocking thing about this killer was that he was only 11 years old.

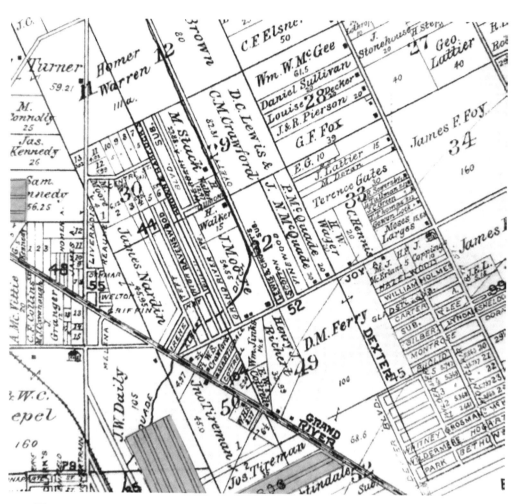

The McQuade family's farm holdings was in what was considered "out in the country" at the turn of century.

Earlier in the day, Hannah had been riding in the two-seat surrey with her sisters and cousins. The McQuade girls were taking their cousins down the Dexter Road so that they could board a streetcar at Grand River Avenue. Hannah's father, Peter McQuade routinely let the girls drive the surrey with an old farm horse that was as gentle as he was reliable.

Shown is a surrey similar to the one that Hannah and the older girls were riding in.

Along Dexter Road, the girls encountered a group of boys who had been roaming the woods shooting birds and squirrels with a little .22 cal Flobert rifle. The boys were from the city of Detroit, and had come out to this farm area where there were places they could shoot the gun and hopefully not get into trouble.

The handsome surrey filled with five giggling girls was more than the boys could ignore, and they jumped aboard it asking for a ride to the city. The girls refused, and the oldest girl, Hannah's sister Myrtle, even cracked the whip at one of the boys to get him to jump off the carriage. The boy with the rifle fired off a shot in an effort to intimidate the girls. Unimpressed, the girls drove the horse on and pushed the unwanted passengers off into the dirt road. The boys regrouped and coaxed their comrade with the rifle to reload and scare the girls again. Buckling under to this peer pressure, he did so and fired a shot in the direction of the carriage.

The unthinkable happened: Surpassing incredible odds, the round struck little Hannah McQuade in the forehead, killing her almost instantly.

The boys scattered as Hannah dropped into the arms of her sister Mary. Stunned, the girls halted the horse and screamed for help. A neighbor was the first to respond, and he carried little Hannah to her home and laid her on the couch. Hannah was white-faced and still, dead before she was received by her mother.

In the county lock-up in Detroit, 11 year old Johnny Goodson cried and explained over and over, "I didn't mean to kill that little girl. I didn't mean to shoot her." Johnny's companions had all been rounded up by police; the Flobert rifle was also recovered. The prosecutor ordered that Johnny be held at least until morning, to be charged or released.

The McQuade farm was astir all night. Women cooked meals and made tea and coffee. Neighbors came and went. Telegrams were sent to family members. The McQuades needed to make funeral arrangements with the undertaker. They needed to choose and pay for a burial plot for their littlest member. Mrs. McQuade was encouraged to get some rest, but she was despondent and could not sleep.

Mr. Peter McQuade told reporters that he was disgusted and sick at heart as to how city folks can allow their boys to come out to the country and cause mischief. And now they are even coming with their firearms, he said, the parents not realizing that they are putting deadly weapons into the hands of their boys. He had four sons of his own and knew that boys could be boys, but to give guns to young ones and allow them to roam unsupervised was a recipe for disaster. Peter McQuade was exhausted, and the sound of his wife crying out could be heard clearly out in the yard. Many of the McQuade family wanted justice, and many of them were calling for 11 year old Johnny Goodson to go to jail for the rest of his life.

In 1905, this portion of Greenfield Township, which was later annexed by the City of Detroit, was indeed out "in the country." Farms, pastures, woods, small creeks and streams abounded. The D.M. Ferry Seed Company held an enormous tract of property near the McQuade farm holdings. The roads were hard-packed, passable in good weather but difficult to traverse in wet weather and in snow. Automobiles were still a rare thing to see. Detroit was not the Motor City just yet. The McQuades were wealthy, and the large family that Hannah was a part of was hard-working and frugal. Hannah had fine clothing, a good education, and she and her siblings lived in a large, well-built home with plenty of farmland to sustain it. The creek nearby was called McQuade Creek, and the McQuades were well known in the area.

What of Johnny Goodson?

Johnny Goodson was from the city. His parents were working class folk, living in a neighborhood of modest homes. Johnny's father was often incapacitated with painful back problems and couldn't work consistently. Johnny was well-liked by his pastor and his schoolteacher. He was not an unintelligent boy, nor was he reckless or troublesome. He was an average All-American boy. How did it come to be that he killed Hannah McQuade, a little girl he didn't even know?

Johnny and his friends from his neighborhood had borrowed the gun from an older boy. They used .22 cal charges to shoot at various targets around their homes. A police officer walking his beat caught them playing with the rifle, and he told them that he would confiscate it if they didn't get out of the city and into the

Flobert rifle.

country to play with it. This is precisely what the boys did and they spent the day in the vast fields and wooded areas of what would become west Detroit.

The prosecutor pondered over all the details, and his fact-gathering had led him to one conclusion, and so Johnny Goodson was charged with manslaughter. The populace was divided about this case. Some sided with Hannah's family and felt that Johnny was capable of murder, and that he maliciously pointed the rifle fully intending to kill someone. Others sided with Johnny and formed the opinion that an 11-year-old playing with a rifle probably just fired off a shot in the direction of the girls' wagon or possibly by accident. Almost everyone agreed though, that if Johnny, in that moment of childish anger wanted to kill someone or not, he didn't understand the concept of the finality of death, and he was truly remorseful that his actions had caused it.

Johnny was kept in custody of the Sheriff, and he was fed and housed in the Sheriff's own home. This was a humanitarian act that the prosecutor did not object to. Of course the boy wanted to go home, and his anguished parents wanted him home, but they were helpless and had to stand by and watch the trial play out.

JOHN GOODSON.   HANNAH McQUADE.

Original newspaper.

The trial did not last very long. Hannah's sisters, her cousins and others testified to the event. Hannah's cousin Blanche Mulcair was particularly bitter and harsh. She testified that she looked at Johnny Goodson as he shouldered and aimed the rifle. Blanche was an outspoken, precocious young lady and her testimony was credible. The courtroom was filled with spectators and interested parties. Johnny sat with his attorney Mr. Robison and his parents. He looked very skinny and forlorn in the big chair in his starched shirt and knickers.

Johnny testified that the shooting was accidental. He said he had put the rifle under his arm. He demonstrated this for the jury. He admitted he had his finger on the trigger and that the barrel seesawed and then he accidentally shot the gun off. Johnny was as repentant and despondent as Hannah's cousin Blanche Mulcair was indignant and scornful.

In the end, Johnny was acquitted.

The courtroom erupted in a frenzy of emotional outbursts.

Johnny was quickly ushered into the judge's chambers. The judge spoke gently to little Johnny Goodson, telling him that he could go home now but that he may be known as "the boy who killed that little girl." The judged urged Johnny to forsake any taunting or bullying he might be subject to in the coming years. He asked that Johnny maintain his dignity and walk away from any teasing. Johnny was released into the custody of his grateful parents.

The courtroom was cleared out, but not before a woman, all in black, spoke aloud to the people as they were leaving. She admonished the jury and the citizens for feeling sorry for Johnny, who, she said, surely had a worthless life ahead of him. She preached loudly that Hannah was a rich girl who had a golden future ahead of her and this was now crushed; ended by a boy who was going to live his life out fully while little Hannah was buried in the cold earth. The woman, in her black veil and in a high voice, cursed Johnny Goodson, avowing that he would surely meet a horrible, untimely death just as sweet little Hannah McQuade had.

Hannah McQuade was buried in her mother's family plot in Mt. Elliott Cemetery. After a few years, Peter McQuade sold and subdivided his farm and it was developed into middle income residential neighborhoods. McQuade Creek was filled in. There are two McQuade subdivisions in the area of Joy Road and Dexter Road, and there is McQuade Street where Hannah's father's farm had been located, just north of Joy Road.

It could have been some consolation to the McQuades that in the final minutes of her life, Hannah was happy and secure in the company of her big sisters. She was laughing and admonishing the boys, "You stay off my papa's carriage!" Hannah didn't suffer when the shot hit her. With her last breaths, she had been jubilant and playful. Her last moments were not in anguish or suffering.

Hannah was looking right at Johnny when he fired. The shot hit her directly in the forehead. Hannah knew whether he had aimed it or not.

Johnny Goodson did go on to live his life. He grew up and became a plumber. He got married. Perhaps he took to heart the curse directed at him when he was only 11 years old. After some marital and financial problems, Johnny Goodson was despondent. He checked in to the Fort Wayne Hotel alone. Shortly afterward, he leapt to his death from the 9th story. He was 34 years old.

It is unknown what Johnny Goodson's last moments were like.

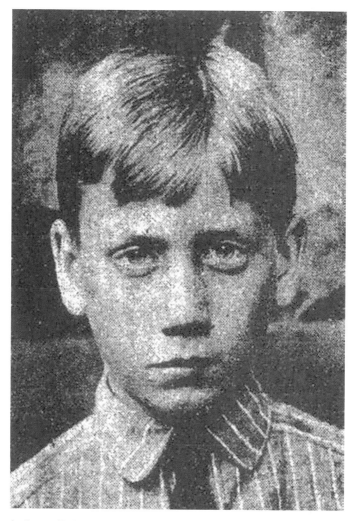

A photo of Johnny Goodson during his trial by a courtroom photographer. His mom would straighten his tie for him in court every morning.

*Portrait of Daniel Thompson
in his later years.*

CHAPTER 6

Battle for Thompson's Tavern

aniel Thompson was born 1787 in Connecticut and was a Dearborn pioneer who came to Michigan in 1824. He was an upstanding citizen and veteran of the War of 1812. He was commissioned by the Northwest Territorial Government to survey and lay out the Chicago Road, now Michigan Avenue. Daniel Thompson liked the area, and set up his homestead on his newly purchased Private Claim 39.

His claim, the oldest in the west end of Dearborn was originally owned by James Cissne, who settled it as early as 1786. This claim, "Private Claim 39" was 134 acres and it ran from northeast to the southwest, beginning at the point where the Lower Rouge River met the Upper Rouge River. This is Michigan Avenue near Evergreen Road in the present day. French "ribbon farms" of the Detroit area were always narrow and always fronted a waterway.

Surveys being what they were in the early 1800s, the junction of the two rivers was not pinpointed perfectly. However, the surveyor's sketches and his written description of the property shows Claim 39 to be at the point where the two rivers meet. James Cissne originally settled the property, improved it, cleared some of the timber and built upon it a rude log dwelling. He then moved to Ohio. Before Cissne could sell the property he had to prove it was his. He was able to confirm his claim with the U.S. government by affidavits submitted by fellow farmers who swore that Cissne never abandoned his claim. Cissne's claim was approved.

By the 1820s, Daniel Thompson built another building in addition to his dwelling-house and called it Thompson's Tavern. He occupied only about 7 acres of the original claim. He also built a stable, barn and had another crude, log building, probably Cissne's original log cabin. Thompson built his little empire on the Chicago Road; both sides of it in fact, and because his property had frontage on the Rouge River, where the Lower met the Upper, Thompson had access to the waterway. The arrival of the Arsenal, just 1/4 west

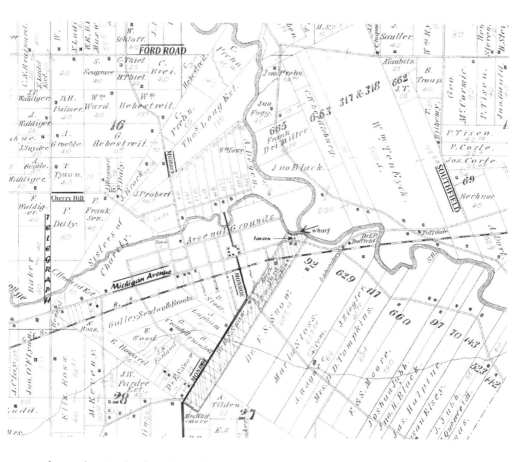

A map showing the place where the Lower and Upper Rouge River meet.
Thompson's private claim number 39 was originally claimed by pioneer
James Cissne about 1786. The shaded area is the claim, and it was purchased
by Dr. Snow and subdivided over the years.

of his property on the Chicago Road was a boon for business. His tavern business was an affable and pleasant place for locals to visit, and for pioneers and settlers to stay overnight in and rest up for their journeys west to their own lands in lower Michigan Territory. Daniel Thompson leased out his tavern for political meetings of the voters in the area of this part of Wayne County. He was known as fair-minded man and a family man.

Joshua Howard was the dashing Lieutenant who was charged with building the arsenal in Dearbornville and who was instrumental in naming the town after Howard's personal hero General Henry Dearborn. He and Stephen Webb made no secret of their mutual enmity for each other.

Joshua Howard, a Lieutenant in the U.S. Army was given the task of surveying, laying out and building the United States Arsenal at Dearbornville. The huge tract of property along the Lower Rouge, about 1,650 acres was already a "military reserve," set aside by the government shortly after 1805. One of the reasons Howard felt the location at the present day Michigan and Monroe block was so ideal is that it had access to the Rouge River waterway, especially the deep part where the two rivers meet at Thompson's property. The river was navigable from Detroit up to that point.

This meant that supplies could be ferried up to the arsenal, bypassing the often impassable Chicago Road and its ruts and thick mud that existed in bad weather.

The army was agreeable with Lieutenant Howard, and in 1833 work was underway on the 11 buildings that would be connected by a 12' high brick wall and within which would be a secure place for the U.S. Army to store, maintain and repair its weaponry for Detroit. Howard worked tirelessly to build the arsenal and the wharf and was the man who re-named the little settlement to Dearbornville, after Howard's personal hero, General Henry Dearborn.

Joshua Howard was the first Commandant of the Dearbornville Arsenal, and when he went into retirement, Lieutenant Colonel Henry Whiting took over. Captain Stephen Webb was appointed the next Commandant in May, 1835. Webb was directed to finish the massive Arsenal project, including the Powder Magazine just outside the arsenal walls, on what is now Michigan Avenue and Brady Street.

An illustration of Thompson's Tavern from the Bark Covered House by William Nowlin.

Howard, like Dan Thompson, liked the area and so he purchased large amounts of property at Dearbornville. Howard built a sumptuous brick home at Michigan Avenue and Haigh Street.

When most citizens were living in rude log cabins with clay fireplaces, Howard was living in his large mansion with several fireplaces, easily the nicest domicile in town. Howard was settled in and raising his family. He was buying parcels of land and re-selling them at a profit. The village of Dearbornville that began springing up around the arsenal assured Howard that his property investments were lucrative.

Pictured here is Daniel Thompson's daughter Caroline Thompson Cochrane Purdy. She and her husband John Cochrane inherited the tavern but she was widowed soon after and then remarried.

The new Commandant Stephen Webb and Joshua Howard were bitter enemies, with many issues dividing them; some political, some personal. Howard kept an eye on Webb's spending and the work being done to complete the arsenal that Howard had started. Howard let it be known that he thought Webb was overspending the government's money and perhaps lining his own pockets with his erroneous accounting. Some of Howard's arguments on this matter seem justified. Of course this didn't sit well with Webb.

Just outside the military's property was Thompson's homestead and tavern. When Webb learned that Daniel Thompson had sold his claim to Howard and that Howard was leasing it back to Thompson, it didn't take a genius to see why: Howard was interested in Thompson's claim because it fronted the Rouge River at the point where the two rivers meet. This is precisely where the U.S. government's wharf was built, to offload brick and supplies for the building of the arsenal. The question was coming to light…who rightfully owned the wharf? The private landowner or the U.S. Government?

For months, Webb communicated to Daniel Thompson that his tavern and barn were on government property, the vast "Military Reserve." Thompson paid no heed because his Private Claim 39 seemed to be airtight. Webb went to the wharf on what was Thompson's land, but which Webb called military property, and removed some of the wood and stone that had been added there to shore up the wharf. Webb called Thompson's occupation of the property a "trespass on government land."

Daniel Thompson, now 50 years old, transferred his lease to his daughter and her husband John Cochrane and they then operated the farm, the tavern and inn.

Webb and Howard squared off, with Howard now accusing Webb of illegal land-grabbing, and Webb accusing Howard of illegally occupying and trespassing on military property, especially the wharf. In one of Webb's letters to his superior Col. Bomford he writes:

August 3, 1837
Captain Howard's chief aim has been to annoy and harass me all in his power and with the aid of his defendants to endeavor to embarrass me in my operations here.

Howard kept on improving the wharf. Cochrane kept the

tavern running. Many a soldier from the arsenal and local citizens found the tavern to be a place of repose and relaxation where a hard working man could enjoy his ale and a tall story or two.

Webb was furious that Howard allowed Thompson's Tavern to keep operating. In 1837 after months of accusations and heated interchanges between the men, Webb sought and successfully obtained a court order for the removal of the structures that were on "government land," no matter what the boundaries of Private Claim 39 were. Webb was basically declaring eminent domain.

The court decision came down in no uncertain terms: Thompson's claim was legitimate, and he had rightful ownership of his property, but NOT the part of his property lying north of the Chicago Road. In effect, not the wharf nor the structures on the north side of Michigan Avenue. Thompson, Cochrane and Howard would not accept a payment for this small parcel of the property that abutted the Rouge, nor would they accept having to vacate it.

Webb set his eyes on the Tavern itself. The stage was set for the Battle for Thompson's Tavern.

On the morning of August 5, 1837, Webb led 50 of his soldiers and laborers from the arsenal and they marched the short distance to Thompson's Tavern. Howard, expecting trouble since being served with the court papers, had stayed overnight in the tavern, and had Cochrane's wife (Thompson's daughter) speak with the soldiers and stall them for as long as she could. Howard rallied the citizens of Dearborn and met the soldiers head on. The soldiers were armed, and also had pikes, poles and rope to pull down the tavern and the other structures illegally situated on government property. Howard's men had clubs and a fierce loyalty to Howard.

The two sides clashed, and the situation turned ugly almost immediately. Webb wrote to his superior:

August 5, 1837

At an early hour this morning I went with my men to the premises, and after they were formally placed in my possession by the civil officers, I directed my workmen to remove the buildings. Capt Howard, with a party of his men attempted to resist the order but after a short struggle, in which he drew a pistol and sword and struck one of my men, he gave way and the workmen are now demolishing the buildings, an old log house and barn.

The scene that day on the Chicago Road had to be one that was not to be missed by the citizenry of Dearbornville. Everyone knew Webb would not be thwarted. Everyone knew that Howard was enjoying his flouting of Webb's authority. When the soldiers came out of the gates of the arsenal and headed downhill to Thompson's Tavern, word spread quickly to supporters and onlookers alike. This was certainly a lot of excitement for 1837.

Some accounts of the Battle for Thompson's Tavern mention the death of citizen named Potter, who suffered a clubbing to his head and who died shortly afterward. Other accounts mention that it was a soldier who was hit in the head and expired of his injury. Neither of these accounts mentions who did the hitting. Perhaps both of these accounts are only partly correct. Had it been true and had it been one of Webb's men who died at the hands of Joshua Howard, in direct resistance to a lawful court order, it is highly doubtful that this murderous act would have been overlooked by Webb and not used to his advantage to prosecute Howard and the protesters. In his letter, Webb admits one of his men was struck by Howard, but perhaps it was a glancing blow and caused no real injury. As it was, Webb prevailed and the tavern was pulled down, its logs tossed into the woods at the incline above the lower Rouge River, about where the restaurant Andiamo's is now situated.

The tavern returned to business, although now housed in a legally situated structure on the south side of the Chicago Road.

The Battle for Thompson's Tavern wasn't over. Joshua Howard kept on with his lawsuits, attempting to recoup the property north of the Chicago Road. He kept on with his letter writing campaign to Washington, bringing to light the discrepancies he thought were in Webb's accounting books. There were many lawsuits initiated between these men and criminal charges launched against Howard. After many hearings and court appearances on both sides, the issues were finally settled two years later.

Although in a legal sense he was the loser, Joshua Howard was successful in bringing to light the need for a more precise examination of the account books of Captain Stephen Webb's. Despite Webb's protests and defenses that he mounted, he assuredly was extremely careful in his accounting because of Howard's persistence. Howard may have lost the tavern and the wharf, but he succeeded in doggedly pursuing Webb and his accounting practices, not to mention being an embarrassing thorn in Webb's side for years.

As the years passed, Daniel Thompson, for whom the Tavern was named, became the Sheriff of Wayne County in 1844. He enjoyed many political positions throughout his lifetime. He was a beloved, prominent citizen and died in 1860 at age 73 and was buried in Elmwood Cemetery in Detroit. His descendants continue to live in the Dearborn area to this day. His tavern is long gone, his property sold, but the legend of the Battle for Thompson's Tavern lives on.

These are hand-hewn timbers from the arsenal dock recovered from the river bank. The dock that was the center of so much controversy in 1837 was unearthed during the construction of the westbound lanes of Michigan Avenue near Evergreen in 1966.

These are Chris Breitenbach's two half brothers, Peter and Matthew, who were little when Breitenbach disappeared. They were both intelligent and were well educated, and as adults they were extremely successful in their business ventures.

CHAPTER 7

A Savage Grandson

e was different than the rest of the family. He was different than his brothers and sisters, and he wasn't the same as his cousins. Everyone in his family was loved, wanted, and more than anything, everyone else belonged.

Born in 1861 in Springwells, Michigan to a 17-year-old unmarried mother, Christian Breitenbach never felt as though he belonged. Chris was the reason his mother married his stepfather. He carried the same name as his younger siblings, but he wasn't one of them, not entirely. He wasn't expected nor wanted and his presence at every family gathering made him, in his mind, feel even more unwelcome.

The rage that built up inside him knew no bounds. He was told that it was his imagination and that he was a good son and that he should proudly claim his place as the eldest. Chris didn't feel proud of anything. Chris hated his name, too, Breitenbach. It wasn't his at birth.

If there was anything Chris could control, it was his determination to be free to do as he pleased. And so he lashed out and misbehaved to get his way. He wanted everyone to be afraid of him. If they were going to let Chris be a part of the family, then he would make them sorry.

He told his stepfather time and time again that he wanted to kill him. This was taken as the rantings of a little boy having a tantrum. However, as Chris grew to be physically larger and stronger than most boys his own age, it started to make folks nervous. He was watched closely and carefully by his mother. The smaller children were afraid of him. Chris could be cruel, unpredictable, and he liked to intimidate his siblings and his Klosen family cousins.

Grandfather Jacob Klosen was not impressed. He could dampen Chris' rage with just a withering look. Whenever the Breitenbachs visited Jacob Klosen in Springwells Township, Chris was always on guard. Grandfather didn't miss anything, and Chris couldn't get away with misbehaving while he was there. Jacob was a strict Catholic and a member of St. Alphonsus Church on Schaefer Road and Warren Avenue. He followed the tenets of the Church and expected his children and grandchildren to do the same. For the most part they did, until daughter Lizzie got pregnant and had Chris. The pastor noted Chris' birth in the church records, and wrote in Latin: Christianus, fil. Illeg. Elisabethae Klosen, natus Die 3rd Nov., B. Die 10th Nov. 1861. "Christian, the illegitimate child of Elizabeth Klosen, born Nov. 3, baptized Nov. 10, 1861."

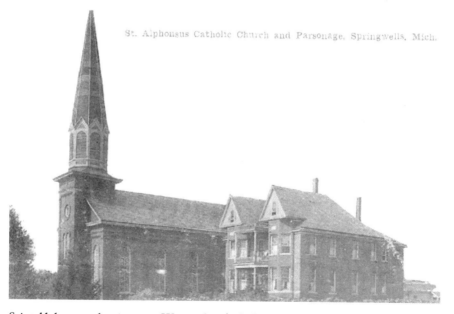

St. Alphonsus Catholic Church and Parsonage, Springwells, Mich.

Saint Alphonsus when it was on Warren Avenue before the church was demolished and rebuilt north of the old location. Jacob Klosen was buried in the church cemetery at Gould and Schaefer Road.

Elizabeth Klosen later married Peter Breitenbach, ten years her senior, when Christian was still a toddler.

By the time Christian Breitenbach was 14, he was well known to the local police and sheriff. He was mainly involved with a gang of tough boys who burglarized shops and railroad cars. Chris enjoyed this immensely. Even when he was caught at times, the police could only charge him with trespassing or having stolen property in his possession.

There was one time when Chris, his gang of juvenile delinquents and some tramps had broken into a railroad car and made off with quite a bit of property that they were able to sell for a tidy sum. The police grabbed Chris, and under pressure Chris' testimony helped convict the leader of his youthful gang and sent the leader to prison. Chris was sure to get out of town after this and wandered about for quite some time. When he returned home, his family was not overjoyed.

The biggest mistake Chris made was stealing from his grandfather, Jacob Klosen.

It was only about $40.00, but he was caught red-handed and it was Grandfather Klosen who caused him to be sent to the State Reform School for juvenile criminals in Lansing.

Fuming for several years under lock and key, there was no reforming Christian Breitenbach.

When he was released he was 17. Eventually he made his way back to the Detroit area, working odd jobs along the way. He looked up his Aunt Mary. She let him stay one night at her home. She fed him and made him a place to sleep. The next night he stopped in at Uncle John Klosen's. He was hospitable, and he also let Christian stay one night.

The next day, Chris turned up at his grandparents' farm in Springwells, near what is now Schaefer Road and Paul Street.

Jacob Klosen had been out selling produce at the market in Detroit. On his way back home he made a few stops. One was at a general store, and another at Schaefer's Six Mile House and Tavern where he had beer or two. Jacob was 64 years old. When he stepped out of the tavern at Schaefer Road and Michigan Avenue, Jacob could see his little farm through the fields. He felt weary, the sun was setting, and he hurried to get home to his wife, Mary. Mary had not been feeling well, spoke little English, and Jacob didn't like leaving her alone too long.

Jacob and Mary Klosen were not well off and were still residing in the original log cabin they had built 25 years earlier. It was small, but cozy, and had two rooms on the first floor and a sleeping compartment in a loft.

Chris was sitting on the back porch of the cabin when Jacob arrived home.

Jacob Klosen was not happy to see his grandson. He feared him and yet he knew that he must not be intimidated by the young strapping lad. Chris explained that he had been released from the Reform School. He asked his grandparents for some basic amenities.

Chris was given supper and he spoke in earnest to his grandmother and grandfather about the legitimate jobs he had held in the past few months. He told his grandparents he had changed his ways and was trying to make it in the world on his own. It was almost 8 p.m. and time for bed. Jacob Klosen told his grandson that he could stay in the barn, not in the house. Jacob was tired from his trek to Detroit. He made his bed on a pallet in the large room on the first floor. Obediently, Chris went to the barn to sleep.

When Jacob retired for the night, he counted the $80.00 he made from the day's market sale. He put the money in his pocketbook and then concealed it in his shirt. He had a secret storage place under a floorboard in the cabin, but with Chris so close by, Jacob didn't trust that his money would be safe unless it was on his person. He soon fell asleep and slept deeply.

Later, Mrs. Klosen answered a soft knock at the kitchen door. Chris complained that it was cold and wet out in the barn. Could he sleep on the floor in the kitchen where it was warm?

Mrs. Klosen, with her heart of gold, could not refuse her errant grandson. She had him bring in a pile of hay from the barn and with a blanket she let him stay in the kitchen. Mrs. Klosen then went to bed in the loft, trying to be quiet so as not to awaken Jacob.

She slept restlessly. Rising before sunrise, she could not shake off a feeling of dread that had come over her. She crept past her husband where he lay in the darkened room and went into the kitchen. Immediately she noticed that Chris was gone. This worried her. Where would he go in the middle of the night? Would he get into more trouble? Was he really "reformed?"

She went in and checked on Jacob. She nudged his shoulder and it was cold and rigid, so she reached and felt Jacob's face. Her hand became immersed in sticky wetness. She lit a lamp and to her horror, found her husband Jacob Klosen with a savage head wound that obliterated half his skull. He was laying face up on the cushioned pallet. Thick, dark blood lay in a pool about his ruined face and had soaked the pillow. In those few terror-filled moments, she knew her husband was dead, his money was gone. She knew that there was no hope for her grandson Christian Breitenbach; that he must be found and he must pay for this unnatural act. He was a monster.

Sorrowfully, she wholly understood the consequences of her

misjudgment. She had trusted Chris, let him into the kitchen, and now her dear husband had paid for her folly.

That next day, Sunday September 1, 1878, there was a flurry of activity at the Klosen's cabin. Klosen grandchildren lingered about outside, and law enforcement officials had combed through the home and property searching for clues. There seemed to be no doubt that the perpetrator of this deed was the victim's own grandson, Christian Breitenbach but the police wanted to be sure. There had however already been a warrant issued for his arrest, and word was spread throughout every city and county police department to be "on the look-out" for him. While police were still at the Klosen home, others were already looking up Breitenbach's old employers and friends for any sign of him.

This is Joseph Schaefer's place, showing the tavern where Klosen and other farmers like him could stop in for meals, beer and to hear news in the community. On the night he was killed, Klosen stopped here briefly but hurried home to be with his sick wife.

Jacob Klosen had been hit once in the head, near his right eye with an ax. There was no ax in the cabin, but police found one just outside the cabin door. It belonged to Klosen and was taken from its place in the woodpile and it was undoubtedly the murder weapon: There were bloodstains and several gray hairs stuck to it.

Sightings of Chris Breitenbach were reported to police. After leaving his grandparents' home, he walked the four miles to the train station in Detroit, asked about schedules and then he purchased a revolver for $9.00 at store near the Grand Trunk Railroad and Michigan Avenue. Mr. Peter Raths, the storeowner, also said that the youth asked where he could buy a new shirt. A shopkeeper who knew Breitenbach also came forward to say that she had sold him a shirt for fifty cents and that he was very nervous, and covered in perspiration. Sunday evening, Breitenbach was spotted in the woods near Lonyo's brickyard near Michigan Avenue and Wyoming Street.

Jacob Klosen supported himself and his wife on 20 acres, and his five children were not much better off. They had to borrow from neighbors and friends to have a suitable funeral for him. Jacob Klosen was given a Catholic funeral from his church. Pastor noted the events in the church records: "Christian, on the night of Sept. 1 as Jacob lay sleeping in his house, struck him in the head with an ax and robbed him of his money. Jacob was buried Sept. 3, 1878."

Apparently the police were correct when they figured that Chris Breitenbach had no feasible escape plan. With nowhere else he could think of to go, the young man headed back toward Lansing to the Reform School. The school officials were notified, and they were waiting for him to show up. He was captured by a Lansing Constable. He was carrying his grandfather's pocketbook. He spoke to reporters when he was brought back to Detroit. Breitenbach claimed his innocence and said that he was surprised to read about the murder in the newspaper.

Chris Breitenbach admitted he was at his grandparents' home and that his grandfather had "pitched into" him, telling him that he was not wanted there. In the evening, his grandfather laid down in his bed. Chris was put out but he did not want to sleep in the barn. He went out and brought in some hay into the kitchen. "After thinking it over, I made up my mind to go away and so I did leave the house a little after 7 o'clock." Christian Breitenbach's defense was going to be that an unknown person killed his grandfather, coincidentally but tragically, just after Chris had walked out.

The trial was held in November, 1878, and Chris Breitenbach was convicted by a jury of second degree murder. The judge sentenced him to life in prison at hard labor. Shortly afterward, Chris was writing home for money to hire an attorney for an appeal. He wrote to his stepfather, "Dear Father, I write these few lines to let you know that I am well. I wrote you two letters before but did not receive an answer." Chris goes on to tell his father that an attorney will file an appeal for him with the Supreme Court but he needed money to do it. His letter continued, "When I get out I will repay you a thousand times, if I have to work day and night to do it...you cannot comprehend how hard it is to be in prison...I am as innocent as a lamb of the charge, and I hope that you will help me once more, and you will not forget me in this hour of need."

Breitenbach didn't get a new trial and he stayed put in Jackson Prison. That is, until February 2, 1882 when he escaped. Years later he had still not been found nor had there been any word from him to his old acquaintances or family. The degree to which his family lived in morbid fear and dread after his escape can only be speculated.

3 o'clock Edition.

THE SPRINGWELLS TRAGEDY.

Further Particulars of the Atrocious Affair.

THE MURDERER TRACKED TO THE VICINITY OF THIS CITY.

And Now Said to be Hiding in the Woods.

This morning a NEWS reporter visited the scene of the Klosen tragedy, which is located about seven miles from the city hall in the township of Springwells. The Klosen place is in full view from the Six Mile house on Michigan avenue. —The house is a small old log cabin, evidently having been built for 20 or 30 years. It contains a large room and small kitchen down stairs and a

The headlines in the Detroit newspapers in the aftermath of Jacob Klosen's murder.

This is the cover of C.D. Hildebrand's book, "18 Years Behind The Bars."
In the book he describes the Hines couple who kidnapped him and raised him
among Indians at Shabbona's Grove, Illinois. Later, Hildebrand would visit
his mother on the Bucklin farm, once appearing in the census under the name
George Hynes.

CHAPTER 8

Who Was C.D. Hildebrand?

he Remarkable Criminal"
"The Unprincipled Rascal"
"The Champion State Prison-ist"

To hear it from Charles D. Hildebrand, he was all these things and more.

Hildebrand was definitely a legend in his own mind, if not in the minds of law enforcement officers and private eyes.

To hear his life story, one must separate fact from fiction in an enormous way, for Hildebrand was also a con man, a scam artist and a known liar.

In newspapers from New York to Chicago, Charles D. Hildebrand was reported to be a shrewd criminal. He was often charged, convicted and sent to prison. But this cunning man was also able to convince reporters to write articles about him that seemed too fantastical to believe.

Hildebrand said he was born in Dearborn Township in 1840 along the banks of the Rouge River. How had this local boy turned to a life of crime?

The first anybody heard of Hildebrand in the newspapers was about 1866. Calling himself William Tompkins, one of Hildebrand's many aliases, he spoke to a reporter from the Milwaukee Daily Wisconsin. The story was picked up by the New York Times. Hildebrand, or Tompkins, is described as a calculating man, small in stature with black eyes and about 27 years old. Hildebrand was in Milwaukee because he had just been sentenced to five years in prison for horse thieving, and a detective who knew him well arrested him in Detroit.

The story he told to this reporter began with Hildebrand's

birth, on Leap Day 1840. As a baby, he was stolen away by ne'er-do-well alcoholic neighbors and taken to live among Indians in LaSalle, Illinois. He entered a life of crime when he was about 8 years old, and Hildebrand related, with his "freebooting" adult accomplices, he traveled to France, England and Canada. In all of these places he was arrested and sentenced to long years in prisons, but with youth on his side, he was often pardoned and deported after serving only a few months.

MY OLD HOME IN MICHIGAN.

Charles Hildebrand was an excellent artist and drew this illustration of the Bucklin Homestead on the banks of the Upper Rouge .

As he got older, Hildebrand traveled throughout the Midwest, practicing the art of pickpocketing, till-tapping, safe-blowing and robbery. He was arrested many times in New York, Pennsylvania, Ohio and Illinois. He also committed robberies in Indiana, Missouri and California. Sometimes he served a portion of his sentences, but most other times he either escaped or was financed by people he called his "pals" to obtain new trials or to bribe officials to set him free.

Hildebrand once obtained money by running a scam on law enforcement officials after some batch of thieves had pulled off a lucrative bank heist in Union City, Missouri. In his book, "Mississippi Outlaws and the Detectives, Don Pedro and the Detectives, the Poisoner and the Detectives" in 1879, Allan Pinkerton, a well-known detective, mentions Hildebrand. He writes how Hildebrand interjected himself into the bank investigation even though he was in no way associated with the real thieves:

"The most important of all the false clues brought out in this investigation was presented by a noted confidence man and horse-thief named Charles Lavalle, alias Hildebrand. I call it the most important, not because I considered it of any value at the time, but because it illustrates one of the most profitable forms of confidence operation, and because the express company, by refusing to accept my advice in the matter, were put to a large expense with no possibility of a return."

Hildebrand told the same life story to a reporter of the Pittsburgh Commercial. He described his birth in Dearborn, his kidnapping by neighbors living near his home, his early years in Illinois, and the sentences for his crimes that he was mostly able to avoid. By this time, he was describing to reporters his incarcerations as being torturous stays with prison guards using fiendish, inhuman techniques to punish inmates. Reporters as well as readers were fascinated with the gruesome details that

Hildebrand described: Being chained, naked, face down to a cold cement floor for weeks at a time. The "shower bath" torture of being nearly drowned, over and over, while standing up and chained into a small tank. He described female inmates as having been brutally sexually assaulted, and women who gave in to such treatment were, for their cooperation, not beaten too severely.

An aerial view from the 1940s shows the property that was Private Claim 615 and purchased and homesteaded by the Bucklins in the 1820s. The property is now River Oaks Estates Subdivision and the Middle Rouge Parkway. Henry Ford once owned all of this property and built a mansion here for his employees, Mr. and Mrs. Ray Dahlinger.

Hildebrand not only talked about his infamous life of crime but of the need for prison reforms because of scenes he witnessed inside the prison cells. How did a local boy get kidnapped, sucked into a life of crime and imprisonment, and then gain even more notoriety by granting interviews with reporters of major papers? What was true and what was Hildebrand confabulating?

His aliases give a clue. He called himself William Tompkins, Charles Montrose, William Henry Harrison, Charles Melville, Charles Lavalle, and in one instance he told a reporter that his real name was William Bucklin.

Starting from the beginning of his life: Hildebrand said he was from Dearborn, 10 miles west of Detroit and 3 miles north of the Village of Dearborn. That would put him right on the vast Bucklin estate.

The Bucklin Family was wealthy and prominent. The Bucklins were pioneers and the township was briefly named Bucklin Township before it was changed to Dearborn. They held a large tract of land, Private Claim 615 of the Michigan Territory, on the banks of the Upper Rouge River near what is now Ford Road and Evergreen. The Bucklins arrived in the area about 1809, and held important public offices, were war veterans, and were well-respected. How did a character like Hildebrand come from such stock? There were no public reports of a missing Bucklin baby.

Hildebrand says that he remembers he was able to learn his name from an old woman who lived on the Indian Reservation at Shabbona's Village. After the people who kidnapped him died, this "toothless hag" told him his origins and his true name and when Hildebrand was almost 8 years old he was given over to a man who promised him passage, by carriage, to go home to his family in Michigan. Instead of conveying the boy home, the man instead dumped him off and abandoned him in some small town. Four days later, the starving and shivering boy met up with the adult criminals who led him into a life of crime.

Hildebrand would never publicly admit his real name or his mother's name and it wasn't until he was 15 that he says he actually went to his mother's house in Dearborn. When he arrived, they did not know him. He explained who he was and then the reunion was tearful and happy. According to Hildebrand, the names of the people who kidnapped him were recognized by his mother. She had certainly mourned his loss and told Hildebrand that she still did not understand why he was taken. While at home along the banks of the Northern branch of the Rouge River, he got to know his brothers and sisters, and spent time with his mother. His father was dead. But soon, the life of crime and the life on the road beckoned to him and Hildebrand again went back to his criminal ways.

The Detroit Free Press reported on him regularly, although not giving him the biographical feature space that other newspapers did. In the 1870s, the Free Press reported that Hildebrand began calling himself a "Reformed Burglar." When Hildebrand offered up to reporters his life story, concluding with his intentions to go straight and to reform, the papers hardly took him seriously. Because Hildebrand earlier self-professed to be involved in heinous murders and train robberies, the news reporters wrote with glee whenever word of another arrest of the "reformed criminal" took place in cities such as Toledo and Cincinnati.

Hildebrand himself offered answers for how he turned out to be a criminal, but in the 1870s at the height of his criminal career, law enforcement was not listening nor did they care.

A November 1871 article in the Northville Record, a Michigan newspaper, referred to a local highway robbery that had taken place. Andrew J. Bucklin, Hildebrand's brother, was arrested because he resembled the robber but was then released. Was it Hildebrand who committed the robbery and did his brother resemble him so much that the two were mixed up?

The police in Detroit hated Hildebrand and when he was in town he was followed around until the police could find some reason to lock him up, including petty charges for vagrancy. Hildebrand kept up with his travels and thieving. Once in 1872, Detroit papers reported that they received a telegraph dispatch that the outlaw Charles D. Hildebrand had been lynched by a mob in Missouri. The Detroit papers said that they think the mob did the right thing and that this was, at last, the end of Hildebrand. They mocked that he certainly had not reformed. Days later, Hildebrand himself showed up at the newspaper office to set the record straight that it was not he who was hanged and that he was "hale and hearty" and stopping by his mother's home for a visit. The man in Missouri who was hanged was a dead ringer for Hildebrand and was using that last name when he was arrested.

"Horse Thief," "Notorious Convict," "Slippery Charlie…"

…so many nicknames Hildebrand had been known by.

Hildebrand bragged that he was sentenced, throughout his life, to 63 years in prison, but had served only 18 years behind bars. What he had always desired was a home to call his own where he would be among family.

Hildebrand kept touting himself, in earnest, as the "Reformed Criminal." In January, 1879 he got married and he went on a lecture circuit throughout Michigan, Ohio and Illinois. He was a talented artist and eloquent speaker, and all who came to see him were enthralled. His artistic talents were put to use by his graphic drawings of the tortures he endured. These illustrations were mounted on a huge roller which was pulled across the stage and illuminated from behind. The "Reformed Criminal" was packing the houses, especially with young boys in attendance. His lectures were not to be missed and he preached to his captivated audience about the atrocities he suffered in prisons and how important it was to never enter into a life of crime

Hildebrand was doing well on the lecture circuit and was living in Ypsilanti with his wife and her three children. In census records, he listed himself as Charles D. Hildebrand, Lecturer. He wrote his life story in a book, Eighteen Years Behind the Bars which was published in 1882.

THE FORM

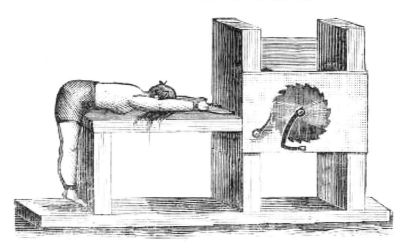

Hildebrand's book is also filled with illustrations of despicable tortures and punishments used on inmates in American prisons. On his lecture circuit, Hildebrand 's shows were well attended.

In the cities where Hildebrand made his rounds, newspapers disparaged him as an "errant humbug" and reviewed his lecture and book by saying it wasn't worthy of dime novel literature and that

Hildebrand merely was telling tales of woe about "his worthless career" and "making considerable money" doing it.

A framed silhouette wedding keepsake made for the Bucklins by an unidentified artist is in the Dearborn Historical Museum Collection.

Hildebrand's book was illustrated by him of course, but he never offered his real family name in it. He also never offered an explanation for his kidnapping. His book was autobiographical in nature but it reads like historic fiction with a lot of drama. He bemoans his lack of an upbringing with his own true, loving family. He decries the use of whiskey which kept him well-rooted in his life of crime. And he denounces the inhumane treatment that prisoners are subjected to in the American prison system.

In Hildebrand's marriage certificate from Illinois, he stated that he didn't know the name of his father but that his mother was Sarah Dunning.

Sarah Dunning married James Bucklin in 1839. James was a 38-year-old widower with several small children and needed a wife. Sarah, age 19, came from a respectable pioneer family in Redford. She was an educated schoolteacher. If Hildebrand was her child and was born in February of 1840, then James Bucklin may not have been his biological father since the wedding was December 1839. Maybe Sarah Dunning needed a husband as much as Bucklin needed a wife and mother for his kids. It would seem to be a win-win situation. James Bucklin and Sarah Dunning had other children together and she was by all accounts a good wife and raised her stepchildren and her own offspring faithfully and competently.

Not completely dismissing the marriage as one of convenience and acknowledging that it may have been one of love and devotion, perhaps Bucklin married Sarah Dunning knowing of the pregnancy and thought the child was his own. Maybe the child was his own. Perhaps other factors later led Bucklin to feel that the child was not his after all. Was he trying to be kind to a young, unmarried girl who found herself in "the family way" or was he the kind of man who could become cruel and vindictive in a vicious way?

Ten years earlier, James Bucklin's widowed father William was in similar circumstances where he'd married a woman named Margaret Tompkins. It was a third marriage for both of them. She promptly had a baby and soon after, William Bucklin threw her out and off the Bucklin lands. When she sued for child support, he stated in court papers that his new wife had never even been properly divorced from her second husband. He refused to support a baby that was not lawfully his. The court ordered him to pay $5 per week until the matter could be straightened out and so William Bucklin began putting all of his assets in other peoples' names including his adult children and his siblings. Before the trial could get underway, William Bucklin died. The divorce and the matter of the support and fatherhood of the baby were dropped.

One theory: Perhaps James envisioned this happening to him and took steps to prevent it. Did he hire people to steal the child?

In Hildebrand's book, he states that at age 8 he was told that it was time that he knew who he was and to go home to his true family in Michigan. Coincidentally, 1848 is the year James Bucklin died. It is possible that the people who held Hildebrand were notified to send the boy home because Bucklin had died. This could have been a figurative "the coast is clear" letter; that the boy would not be in danger any longer from his mother's husband.

Maybe it was Sarah Dunning Bucklin who sent the baby away with the neighbors and it was she who gave the all clear sign when her husband died.

Because Hildebrand did not include information on his marriage certificate nor in his book about the identity of his father, it begs the question if Hildebrand even knew for sure the identity of his biological father. The law was clear in those days as it is today: A child born in a marriage is assumed to belong to the husband, and must be supported by the husband. Maybe Hildebrand did not want to name his real father if it was in fact not James Bucklin. Maybe in later years he did not want to dredge up the past, cast aspersions upon his mother and relive the heartbreak.

Hildebrand was living in Evansville, Indiana when he died of typhoid pneumonia in 1887 at age 47. It is not known if he stayed in contact with the Bucklins.*

If Hildebrand's father was not James Bucklin, perhaps it was a man named Tompkins, as this alias was one he used most often. Margaret Tompkins Bucklin, the third wife of James' father William, had an adult son by her first marriage. He would have been just about Sarah's age in 1839 and in fact lived on the farm next door. Did Sarah fall for the Tompkins boy, become pregnant by him, and was then married to James Bucklin?

No one may ever know who "The Outlaw" Hildebrand really was, who his father was or which facts of his life may have been embellished with extra drama or charm. He was a local boy from Dearborn, a child of pioneers, and he was certainly born into a situation not of his own making. He said that his heart's true desire was to be an honest man, make an honest living, and have a happy home. Raised by abusive alcoholics and thrust so young into a criminal lifestyle, "The Great Outlaw Charles D. Hildebrand" hardly stood a chance.

In the years that followed, Sarah Dunning Bucklin married Amos Cole and had more children by him and he had children of his own. The biological Bucklins did not want to have the family homestead and huge estate pass into the hands of their stepmother's stepchildren. Sarah's biological children by Cole felt they had a lawful right to the property.

Sarah began dividing it to pay her bills, especially after Amos Cole died, a "hopelessly insane" alcoholic. Eventually all the property, 400 acres, was divided and then either inherited or sold. Later on, Henry Ford bought it all and it became part of his vast estate Fairlane. The property where the farmhouse was situated is where Henry Ford built a mansion for his alleged mistress, Evangeline Dahlinger, 100 years after the Bucklins settled on it. But that's another story.

JOSEPH H.
FOWLER
PVT. 3 BRIG.
MICH MIL
BLACK HAWK WAR

Joseph H. Fowler's tombstone is in a cemetery in Kellogg's Grove Cemetery in Illinois. This burying ground is registered by the National Park Service as a historic place. It is the site of two skirmishes between the militia men and Indians under Blackhawk's direction. Fowler was killed in an Indian ambush. There are 19 graves here.

CHAPTER 9

The Fate
of The Fowlers

ear Sir,
About the year 1831 or a little later, a young man
and his wife by the name of Fowler died in Dearborn
leaving three little girls..."

When Minnie Murphy wrote this letter to the Dearborn Postmaster in 1921, she had hoped that someone in the town could help her locate her ancestors, the Fowler Family. Minnie Murphy, along with her mother Clara Ferris remembered small bits of family lore. Clara Ferris, age 63, could only remember that her mother spoke of her own childhood days as an orphan, raised by a kindly woman whose name no one knew.

These descendants of the Fowlers were now in Texas, and though many years had passed since the pioneer days in Michigan, they hoped, by writing the letter, to solve the family mystery before any record or memory of them disappeared entirely.

"Some woman, presumably a relative, took these girls and cared for them..."

Minnie Murphy didn't know what happened to the Fowler Family, but what she did know was that 90 years earlier, around the 1830s, the Fowler parents died. No one knew exactly when or how they died, or where they were buried. Subsequently, the three little Fowler girls were raised by someone else. Mrs. Murphy knew little else except that the name of the little village of Dearborn seemed to loom large in this family legend.

"I am trying to find out the full name of the parents and the name of the woman who cared for the children. The date is recent enough so that an aged inhabitant could recall it."

Mrs. Murphy was hoping that there was still a trace of the Fowlers, her great-grandparents, in someone's memory:

"I thought, perhaps, if the parents of Mr. Henry Ford were living, they might remember...Any information you can obtain will be appreciated."

After the Murphy letter appeared in the local newspaper, a few replies from Dearborn made their way back to Texas. A local historian was able to find the name of an early Dearborn pioneer named Joseph Fowler. Some weeks later another letter arrived from Mrs. Murphy:

"My Dear Sir,
Your letter received today. It was just what I wanted. Mr. Fowler died before Dearborn was called Dearborn, but it was in that particular locality he lived. Your letter confirmed what my mind faintly recalled, the name Joseph."

But back in 1921, Minnie Murphy and her mother probably never found out what happened to the Fowlers.

Another 90 years has passed since Mrs. Murphy wrote her letter to the Dearborn Postmaster. In this modern day of vast internet genealogical databases the Fowlers from 180 years ago should have been easy to track down. Unfortunately they were not. Early land records show a Joseph H. Fowler living south of Dearborn in the 1820s. Other records show he was a veteran of the U.S. Army, and originally hailed from Massachusetts. This would indicate that the Fowlers arrived before Michigan became a state, and before the Erie Canal opened. The Fowlers must have travelled to Michigan over land. Slogging through the vast Black Swamp of Ohio had to be a journey they would never forget.

Census records from the 1830s show the Fowlers living in the area south of present-day Dearborn. His wife Maria Fowler was a Kilbourn, from another early Dearborn pioneer family. All were settled on the Rouge River south of Michigan Avenue. Joseph

Fowler held several official volunteer positions in the fledgling township of Pekin and Bucklin. From these older townships would emerge the Village of Dearborn.

In order to track the Fowlers, one must examine the First Methodist Church that had its roots in Michigan along the Rouge River in 1810. Seven Methodist families in the Dearborn area gathered in their homes to hold services. In 1818 they built a log church on a piece of land donated by the Sargent Family at what is now Greenfield and Butler Road in Dearborn. By 1828, the Methodist core group were again meeting in their homes, and then these families decided to leave the Dearborn area and branch out.

They went to Branch County. The families included the Tibbets, Corbuses, Abbotts, the Hanchetts, McCartys, and a few others. By 1834, more families living in the vicinity of the Methodist Church had also moved to Branch County. The Fowlers were one of them.

Apparently the Fowler family was intact when they left Dearborn and started down the Chicago Road and re-settled in Girard, Branch County. The family consisted of Joseph and Maria Fowler and at least two daughters, Ann and Pauline.

Friend and fellow Methodist John Corbus had died rather young, having been run over by the cart wheel on his wagon during one of his supply trips to Detroit. Amputation of the leg was necessary, and it was reported as "awkwardly performed," and Corbus died. Branch County probate records show that his estate was indebted to pay Mrs. Fowler the sum of $7.00. Also, by 1833 the land records in Branch County show Maria Fowler as sole landowner of the land Joseph purchased. Joseph H. Fowler's name is conspicuously absent from his family's important matters. Probate records for Maria's relative Johnson Kilbourn shows that Maria and Joseph were both dead by 1836.

Branch County history records show that during the Black Hawk War of 1832, Joseph H. Fowler had signed on as a private in the Michigan Militia Third Brigade. Blackhawk, a Sauk Indian who was extremely angry about the treaties that resulted in the Indians having to cede land east of the Mississippi rallied other Indian tribes and revolted against what he called fraudulent treaties. Blackhawk felt that the white man's spoken words and words that were written down on paper were two different things. In Illinois, Blackhawk rallied disenfranchised Indians to fight to gain back the lands they gave up. Horror stories emerged from the

Black Hawk, war chief of the Sauk.

frontier lands of Illinois about Indians massacring defenseless settlers. Stories of their brutal mutilations of the bodies of their victims, women and children included, planted terror in the hearts of pioneer families. The United States sent troops to quell this rebellion and prevent a wider outbreak of war.

In the end, by 1833, the U.S. troops had prevailed. This war lasted only long enough for both sides to engage in several battles and skirmishes.

Did Joseph get sent to the war Illinois? Did Joseph ever return home?

His daughters were very young when he mustered in. Ann was 8 years old, Pauline was about 2 and Nancy wasn't even born yet. What happened to Joseph and what happened to Maria and their daughters?

Records do show that the three girls survived and all three were married. Ann married a Branch County man, Edward Davis, and moved to Kalamazoo. Pauline went with them. Nancy married a man named Harris, but after having a daughter she named Ann Jane, Nancy was either divorced or was widowed from Mr. Harris. Nancy then married a man named Dickenson, who also could have been from Branch County, and whose family may have been the ones who took the three orphaned girls in when their mother died. Mr. and Mrs. Charles Dickenson moved to the Detroit area by 1880, and by 1890 they were raising Nancy's grandson, Charles Griffiths, whom they adopted and renamed Charles Dickenson.

Sisters Ann and Pauline stayed in Kalamazoo and settled down with their husbands and families, Pauline having married a Mr. John Clarke.

Later, Pauline moved to Texas and died there in 1913. Her

daughter, Clara and granddaughter Minnie undoubtedly were the recipient of many tales told by Pauline about their pioneer days in Dearborn, Michigan. Her mother didn't have all the facts, for she was so young when she was orphaned. Perhaps Clara only listened to the tales half-heartedly. Later in life Clara wanted to know more about her parents and grandparents. The name of the town of Dearborn came to her mind time and time again.

In these early days, a newspaper was an excellent way to get news to the masses. When Mrs. Murphy's letter to the Dearborn Postmaster appeared in the paper, many residents were intrigued. It is not known exactly what transpired but a few weeks later Mrs. Murphy was thanking the citizens of Dearborn for their help, especially a Mr. Frieling, a local history buff. Just receiving information that the Fowler Family was headed up by Joseph Fowler was a great revelation for the ladies.

"Your letter confirmed what my mind faintly recalled, the name Joseph."

One can only wonder still what happened to Maria Kilbourn Fowler. How did her children end up in the care of another family and if Mrs. Fowler did not die, how had the story that she had died become part of the family lore? Was she sick or otherwise indisposed to take proper care of her daughters? Or did she succumb to one of many types of deadly diseases that plagued the pioneers; cholera, tetanus, diphtheria, tuberculosis or smallpox. Perhaps she suffered an accidental death, like hapless John Corbus?

What is true is that Joseph Fowler was a married man, a true pioneer, and he signed on to fight the war against an Indian Uprising. He left his hearth and home, a wife and two daughters and child on the way to do so.

The ladies in Texas seemed to have no information about the

Fowlers moving to Branch County because they had no idea where they were buried:

"Perhaps the names of the parents might be obtained from the tombstones, as they are buried in Dearborn."

Joseph H. Fowler does have a gravestone, and it is in Illinois. He went to war and never returned. He is buried in a plot in Kellogg's Grove cemetery in Stephenson County Illinois, a casualty of the Black Hawk War. Most accounts on record show that Fowler died in the Second Battle of Kellogg's Grove on June 25, 1832. Native Americans under Blackhawk's direction ambushed and attacked the small group of militia men in the woods, and, after a few hours of assault, the Indians withdrew. Five militia men had been killed. These unfortunate men were buried, but not without honors, for Abraham Lincoln, then 23 years old and a volunteer in the Illinois Militia, arrived with his men after the battle to find and bury the dead. This was to be Lincoln's only personal experience in the military and he would never forget the gruesome sight of the dead soldiers and the blood and wounds where they had been scalped. The battle site is registered with the U.S. National Register of Historic Places.

The Fowlers back in Michigan had to learn to make their way without Joseph. The great sorrow this expectant young mother must have endured, to have received word that her husband had been killed! How heartbreaking for her to think on the manner of his death, but how reassuring it must have been to think of his courage in the face of such danger.

The girls were taken in by a foster family, but their names were not erased and they remained Fowlers until they married.

Only Maria's fate is the last mystery. The Fate of the Fowlers has still not completely been determined.

Peter Ford was photographed by one of his
Lapham family customers. He carried all
he needed. Was he a Civil War veteran?
He would never tell.

CHAPTER 10

A Different Famous Ford

obody knew where Peter Ford came from. Nobody knew why he was the way he was. But he was well known in Dearborn, Inkster, Springwells, and Taylor. "Ol' Pete" as he was called, didn't travel fast; he had a game leg and the horse pulling his cart was very old. To see him coming down Michigan Avenue was a wondrous thing: A man with a long matted beard, filthy overcoat and dirty face, worn out shoes, carrying a big burlap bag on his shoulders.

He was a tinker by trade and the housewives knew to get their broken things out for Pete to fix when they saw him coming. In the 1880s, people didn't throw things out when they were broken. Back then things were patched, fixed or repurposed. Pete fixed 'em all. With his irons, hammer, files, resin and solder he fixed everything from large buckets and pots and pans to small dishes.

Resident Henry Haigh described him as "a curious, much-crippled, travelling tinker who lived in a funny old tumble-down canvas-covered cart, drawn by a moth-eaten, pot-bellied, wheezy old horse."

Pete's rather repulsive appearance didn't hinder his business. He was well-spoken if given a chance to carry on a conversation. "His conversation was correct, never forced upon you but weird and interesting if listened to. His imagination embraced the universe." Haigh recalled.

Some folks tried to clean Ol' Pete up. His clothes were layered rags that he would put on and never take off, never launder. His beard was tangled and knotted up. But Ol' Pete liked himself just the way he was, and no one could change him. No one knew why he had chosen this itinerant lifestyle.

He wasn't homeless; he had a dozen "homes" in the area.

He stayed in a woodshed at the rear of Frank Fukalek's shoe store near Michigan Avenue and Oakwood. He slept on the floor of the Brainard's kitchen, near the stove, when he was travelling up towards Ford Road and Telegraph. An abandoned house on Jim Daly's property near Michigan Avenue and Beech Daly was offered to Ol' Pete and it served him well until the owner rented it out to paying customers. He lived in his cart down by the river on warmer days. Pete was also known to "warm" himself in the local saloons and taverns along Michigan Avenue. Soft-spoken and non-violent, Pete was never not welcome.

Shown is Frank Fukalek's shoe store on Michigan Avenue. He had a shed near Oakwood and Michigan that he let Ol' Pete bunk down in, especially in the winter.

"Some people thought that perhaps he had committed some crime and used the outfit to cover up" said resident Samuel Lapham, but he hardly believed that himself. Lapham was a good customer of Pete's, as was Elba Howe, the undertaker, who had Pete repair all kinds of household things like pans and umbrellas. Pete used to even go up on his customers' roofs to repair eaves troughs and drainpipes.

Some folks believed that Ol' Pete was a Civil War veteran and that his game leg was the result of a battle wound.

After Pete fell off his cart one day and broke his game leg, it couldn't be set right, and so his days of climbing up on to houses were over. He acquired a more severe limp this way, but he got along regardless.

Resident Lois Smith said she remembers Pete camping down in the woods by the Lower Rouge River near Michigan Avenue and Inkster Road. The tinker sharpened her family's knives and mended their pans. The kids were afraid of him, but he used to make small sets of play dishes for the girls with his scrap metal. Resident Mildred Cronogue remembered that someone along Michigan Avenue had loaned out their little red-painted shed for Pete to stay in now and again, and she also remembered that he made little tin dishes for the children.

No one knew where he came from but everyone speculated on what would become of him. They figured he would either be found dead one day or he would end up at Wayne County General Hospital and Poorhouse for indigent patients, otherwise known as Eloise. So often even family members could not care for their ailing relatives. When a person's plight came to the attention of law enforcement officers, and it was deemed that they could no longer care for their basic needs or pay their bills, they were "given a ticket to the Poorhouse." The Michigan Central Railroad that ran through Dearborn did make a stop opposite of the Wayne County Hospital grounds. If you were given a ticket, then you were escorted on to the train. When the train made the stop at the Poorhouse, someone from Eloise met you and escorted you to your new "home."

Of course as Pete grew older and feebler, folks began to worry when they didn't see him on Michigan Avenue as much. One day, Ol' Pete's horse keeled over and died. Pete tried to pull his cart around by himself, but just couldn't do it. He started carrying his things in bundles over his back, but he couldn't manage it anymore. They say that Pete fought it when he was given his ticket to ride to the Poorhouse. In 1900, the census records show him still living there. He is listed as a tinker, 69 years old and widowed. The record shows him as having been married, for 6 months, at some time in his life.

Peter Ford got sick at Eloise in 1906, and for three weeks suffered with pneumonia until it finished him off. He was buried in the County Cemetery. Ol' Pete rests in an unmarked grave in this cemetery just off Michigan Avenue, his favorite trading route filled with his loyal customers.

These handmade tin dishes are in the Dearborn Historical Museum's holdings. They were donated by a family who were good customers of Ol' Pete. This family resided on Michigan Avenue between Oakwood and Brady near the railroad tracks. They had two daughters who often pestered Pete for toys.

This is Michigan Avenue after the turn of the century, where Ol' Pete walked and plied his trade. This view is from about Tenny Street looking East.

A photo of Alanson Thomas' son Lorenzo and his wife Rebecca about 1880.

CHAPTER 11

Black Swamp Thomas and Tonquish

The Thomas bothers were a hearty bunch of young men; true pioneers who came to this area in the early 1800s. Alanson Thomas, born in 1788 was known as "Black Swamp" Thomas. When folks were migrating west and staking their claim in the Michigan Territory, they hired Thomas to guide them through the Black Swamp of Ohio, a formidable obstacle of mud and marsh covering 1,500 square miles. If pioneers from the east wanted to get to their land claim in Michigan, they had to spend weeks trudging through the marshes in Ohio to do it. "Black Swamp" Thomas was the man to call on.

The Great Black Swamp of Ohio was a difficult barrier for pioneers coming to their new homes in Michigan from the East. Thickly forested, and teeming with mosquitoes, the black loamy water was present year round and could be chest-high in some places.

Alanson Thomas and his brothers Joel and Aaron lived on property along the Rouge River on the north and south side of The Great Sauk Trail, also known as Michigan Avenue. The Thomas brothers were tenacious, hard-working, and unafraid of the harsh life and dangers they faced in the unsettled areas of what would become Dearborn.

They were veterans of the War of 1812, and after General Hull's Surrender of Detroit, the Thomases briefly re-situated their families, for safety reasons, to Ohio. In May1819, Indians that had previously dwelt in the Detroit area were, by treaty, living on reservations. Many of the Chippewa, Pottowatomie and other bands lived on the Upper Rouge River near what is now 9 mile road. This did not mean that the Indians were happy about this new living

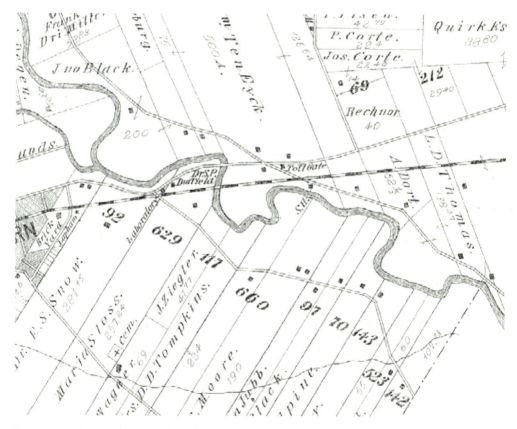

This is a map showing Lorenzo Thomas' land, east of Fairlane Town Center, at present day Greenfield Road and Rotunda Drive.

arrangement. Many Indians felt disenfranchised and could not and would not give up their traditional free-roaming lifestyles. This lead to unpleasant encounters between pioneer settlers and Indians. In particular, a small band of Pottowatomie travelled up and down the Rouge River from 9 mile road to the Detroit River. This band, led by Chief Tonquish, visited settlers' cabins when the menfolk were sure to be out in the fields at work. Intimidating the housewives, the Indians could walk right into their homesteads, demand a meal, and take provisions, tools or anything else they coveted. The terrified pioneer women never balked.

Tonquish was tough and demanding, and his son was just like his father. Rarely meeting with any opposition, they were free to take what they needed and move on. Pioneer men resented them, but, being outnumbered, they did not often resist them. The settlers' homes were so few and far between, they could hardly get up enough manpower to drive off the Indians, much less stop their depredations.

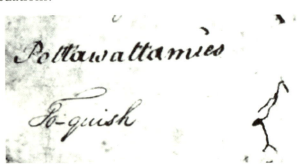

Tonquish' mark on an Indian Treaty. The mark is the symbol of his name and/or its meaning, and closely resembles a long-legged water bird, perhaps a crane or heron.

Complaints to the federal officials in Detroit did not fall on deaf ears. The U.S. Government knew of the tensions between the Indians and the pioneers and would punish either side if crimes were committed and if the guilty parties were brought to them.

This was not an easy thing to do. How do a handful of pioneers and settlers arrest and escort of band of Indians, as prisoners, from the outlying areas like Dearborn to federal officials in Detroit?

The Thomas Brothers' homes were easy targets for Tonquish, since they lay right along the banks of the Rouge. Alanson Thomas' wife was called on by Tonquish and his men one day. The Chief walked into the log cabin uninvited and unannounced, and began to pick up tools he saw that he planned to make his own. Mrs. Thomas gasped out loud at the sight of the Chief in her kitchen. Like so many other times, Tonquish continued helping himself to what he wanted. What Tonquish didn't know was that Alanson was at home that day. He burst into the kitchen and demanded of the Chief, "What are you doing here?"

Tonquish took an offensive stance and lunged at Thomas. Sturdy, fearless Alanson Thomas punched the Chief in the face so hard that he was knocked to the ground. Thomas worked the Chief over, and then dragged him out of the cabin. The cabin was on high ground, and Thomas rolled the semi-conscious Tonquish down the hill towards his men who sat on their ponies.

None of the Indian men would take action. This was their way: Win or lose, a man fought his own battles. But Tonquish' son was having none of seeing his father beaten and humiliated. Infuriated, he called upon the other Indians to aid him in teaching Thomas a lesson and avenging their Chief. But the Indian men stayed out of it. Thomas stood his ground. Seeing the situation out of his control, Tonquish' son hissed to Thomas, "By and by, you will be dead!"

Alanson Thomas answered, unwavering, "Alive or dead, I'll still give you a flogging."

The Indians moved on.

They also avoided the Thomas farm from then on. The next time they visited a settler, it was near Thomas' lands. They stopped at the Sargent farm. The Indians demanded bread of Tom Sargent's wife. A hired man ran to get Sargent and some other men who were working in the fields. When Sargent got to his farm, his wife was terrified and although she had given the Indians all she had, they were demanding more. Sargent's dog ran up and grabbed one of the older Indian's leggings, and the Indian went to shoot it. Sargent quickly grabbed his dog and started to lead him to the cabin to lock him up. Tonquish and his son demanded the dog. An older Indian with the group told Tonquish to let the matter rest. But Tonquish' son threatened Sargent with his gun. Tom Sargent made a run for his cabin and was shot in the back between the shoulders and mortally wounded. Sargent's wife and mother screamed and ran to his aid. The Indians rode off hastily north up the Rouge River.

When the alarm went out, Alanson Thomas, now well-acquainted with Tonquish and his men, answered the call for help. After all, Sargent was a neighbor and a good friend. Thomas immediately joined a posse of pioneers who were now fed up by the intrusions and thefts. All the more enraged by the shooting, Thomas and the other pioneers armed themselves and gathered as many men as they could and went after Tonquish' band. Most of the men in the posse were farmers but almost all had many years' service in the U.S. Army. Under the direction of Major John Macomb, the posse also consisted of William and James Bucklin, Amos Gordon and a few others. They tracked the Indians northward on the banks of the Rouge River, and then west following a creek on the river's middle branch. After one day and one night of pursuit, the pioneers finally caught up with Tonquish' band. These Indians gave themselves up freely, wanting no guilt on their heads for the shooting of Tom Sargent. But Tonquish and his son were not among the others. They were far up ahead of the posse, fleeing through the woods of what is now Westland, Michigan.

When Macomb, Alanson Thomas, James Bucklin and the

others were able to catch up to and physically restrain Tonquish, they saw Tonquish' son in the distance. He would not surrender to the posse. When they leveled their weapons at him, Tonquish stopped them. He told the pioneers that he would call to his son and tell him he must give himself up. When Tonquish called out, in his own language, it was obvious that he had instead directed the young man to run away as fast as he could. Tonquish' son did just that. The Chief said, "Well, he is not coming, go and shoot him." not realizing that his son was still in deadly range of the posse's guns. The Chief saw his son fall under the barrage of gunfire, clearly dead.

Tonquish, infuriated, pulled a knife and sprang onto Macomb as he reloaded. James Bucklin caught hold of Tonquish just in time, and fought him off with the butt of his rifle while Macomb hastily reloaded. Chief Tonquish then also attempted to affect his own escape but was shot and killed. He and his son were buried where they fell. Their graves are there to this day. The creek that is nearby is now named Tonquish Creek.

As time went on more and more pioneers settled the lands of Wayne County and beyond. The Thomas families stayed in Dearborn, and Alanson Thomas' offspring continued to farm his lands. Jackson Thomas, his descendant, was a WWI veteran and afterward became a Dearborn Police Officer.

Thomas Sargent, the last man to be killed by an Indian in Wayne County left behind a wife, a young son Philip, and a mother. His brother John stepped in to care for them.

The Macombs and the Bucklins, also War of 1812 veterans stayed in the area as well. The city of Dearborn emerged from the lands these men cultivated.

Alanson Thomas' descendants have never forgotten him or his tenacity and courage in the face of the hardships of pioneer life.

However, Black Swamp's descendants are even more proud to tell the story of how he squared off with the Pottowatamie Chief Tonquish in the kitchen of his log cabin almost two hundred years ago. He could have suffered the same unlucky fate as Tom Sargent. But Dearborn pioneer Alanson Thomas, alone and unarmed, stood his ground. He defended himself from an attack by an Indian Chief, confronted that Chief's mounted band and live to tell about it.

This is the first page of Tom Sargent's will, written after he was shot. It states," In the name of God, amen. I, Thomas Sargent of the River Rouge, and Territory of Michigan, being very sick and weak, but of perfect mind and memory, thanks be given to God, calling to mind the mortality of body and knowing that is appointed for all men to die, do make and name this my last will and testament..."

In 1948 during road construction behind the Dearborn Inn, human remains were found near a dried creek bed. The oldest residents in town remembered that the Big Sloss Cemetery, also called Pepper Road Cemetery was located here. Thirty years before this discovery it was thought that all of the bodies were removed.

CHAPTER 12

Skeletons and Bone Orchards

n Michigan during the 1800s, hardy pioneers brought all they could carry to their new land, giving up comforts they had known in their home states of New York, Connecticut and Massachusetts. Living hardscrabble lives in the untamed lands without neighbors close by, they faced illness and even starvation in wintertime. Rampant diseases wiped out whole families, even whole settlements and villages.

Most pioneers were farmers who worked hard to eke out a living. When they died, their bodies were buried on their lands. Even after large cemeteries were founded and established, many folks still utilized their community burial grounds, often small and intimate and generally right near their village or settlement. Some had their own family burial grounds, usually located on their homestead land, and cared for and maintained by the family.

When Detroit was growing larger and annexing many small villages and towns, streets and roads were improved and large farms subdivided into lots and sold off. Most small burial grounds or family cemeteries were well known in their respective locale, and they were "vacated," which means that someone undertook the task and expense of digging up the bodies and making arrangements for reburial. Wooden markers and many made of stone did not survive the ravages of time.

What happened to folks who died in transit across the wilderness of Michigan? More than likely they were buried right where they dropped. Without these places being documented, one can only imagine all the places beneath our feet, to this day, that may yield a burial spot from long past, long forgotten and containing the remains of some early resident.

When the City of Detroit began digging "modern" sewers in the mid 1800s, and setting foundations for large brick buildings, homes and hotels, the people were also filling in creeks and grading down hilly areas. They leveled structures that were remnants of older days. They moved cemeteries from the heart of the growing city to well-established cemeteries like Woodmere and Elmwood.

The Chovin Cemetery graves are now in Northview Cemetery. The upright stone is a marker to the people whose graves were moved from the Chovin Cemetery when the property was being developed. Henry Ford paid for the removals and the new stone.

However, they never found every burial. Years, and even decades later, bodies were still turning up when streets were being re-routed and widened, and buildings being razed. Workers who found these skeletons were shocked and sometimes superstitious about disturbing the dead. Some men would walk off the job.

Some of the skeletons were found interred in wooden coffins, and some skeletons still bore the trappings of a French farmer or a British soldier. In the vicinity of the old Detroit "city cemetery," long after it was vacated and all the bodies were moved, graves were unearthed. One grave held the skeleton of a woman with what appeared to be two skeletons of tiny newborns, no doubt a mother and babies who perished in childbirth or shortly afterward. It is believed that folks without the financial means to pay for a plot would steal into the cemetery by night and hastily bury their loved ones in a shallow hole or on top of an established grave.

This is a portrait of Dr. Thomas Haigh whose family claimed him from the Big Sloss Cemetery and re-interred him at Northview. "Tommy" Haigh had to be dug up one more time in his stay at Northview when the family plot inside the cemetery was established.

In the Dearborn area, there were also burial grounds that were neglected. With no family to tend to them, grave markers often were lost and sunken in the earth or simply disappeared over time. Behind what is now the Dearborn Inn was a local burial ground called Big Sloss Cemetery. Maps also show it to be named Green Oak Burying Ground and Pepper Road Cemetery. Henry Haigh, whose wealthy family established Northview Cemetery, came to dig up the body of his brother Thomas Haigh for reburial in Northview. Thomas

Haigh had died young. Haigh describes the event:

"We opened Tommy's grave and took out all that was left of his remains, a few pieces of the coffin and the bones. The coffin plate was in almost perfect condition, bearing the inscription:

"Thomas Haigh M. D. Died June 18, 1871. In the thirty-first year of his age."

We put all into an old chest, put the plate on the chest, fastened down the lid and brought it home.

Tomorrow Father & George will bury the remains in the Haigh lot in Northview Cemetery.

Pit in Springwells.

Considerable excitement was created in the Sixteenth Ward yesterday by a ghastly find made in a sand pit on the Reeder farm near Lovers' Lane.

DISCOVERY OF HUMAN BONES

Recalls a Murder.
About the middle of last week some men discovered a human skull two feet below the sur-

Mysterious Skeleton Found.
Parts of a badly decomposed skeleton have been dug up in River Rouge village, in a spot where no cemetery ever existed, so far as is known, J.

SKELETONS UNEARTHED

ONE DUG UP NEAR THE STATE SAVINGS BANK CORNER.

PROBABLY THAT OF AN AMERICAN WHO FOUGHT WITH PERRY.

Another Was Found in the Old Russell Street Cemetery.

SOMEBODY'S BONES.

The finding of skeletons is always news.

I feared this task might be unpleasant or gruesome, but it was not so. All the flesh was gone from the bones, but the hair and beard remained, and was in perfect shape as Tommy wore them. We almost thought that we could have recognized him from these alone."

The pioneers who owned this burial ground off Oakwood Boulevard were the Sloss family, but it may have been established by early pioneer Hugh McVay in 1830. This cemetery was vacated by an order of the local officials in 1914, as it was going to be sold. The oldest residents in town testified at a town meeting. Mr. Samuel Long remembered the last burial to have been at least thirty years prior to 1914. The cemetery was described as being less than an acre in size, with no boundary markers and only 7 or 8 tombstones still standing. Anyone who had family there and knew where the graves were then came and retrieved their loved ones' remains and deposited them in an established cemetery. The town officials established a general fund to remove and re-inter all the unclaimed bodies.

The stones that were readable were used to determine where the bodies were, and all the bodies that could be found were transferred elsewhere, most to Northview Cemetery. Undertaker Elba Howe was hired to retrieve bodies of his friend John Alexander's two late wives. Howe could only find the remains of the second Mrs. Alexander, but nothing of the earlier wife. These were also reburied in Northview.

However, as late as 1948, skeletons were still being unearthed. On the grounds of Ford Motor Company at the rear of the Dearborn Inn, workers uncovered the skeleton of what appeared to be a white male. This had been precisely the location of the Big Sloss cemetery. There were also metal handles found that probably once were attached to a coffin. Once again, it seems that well meaning folks thought they had found and removed all the graves years before.

The only known photo of Big Sloss Cemetery.

After this discovery at the Dearborn Inn, workers with modern earth-moving equipment discovered another skeleton the next day, this one with patches of red hair stuck to the skull. Red hair was known to have been found in the McFadden and Ross families, who had indeed buried their ancestors at the Big Sloss cemetery, and then supposedly had them moved to Woodmere Cemetery in Detroit. Was this red-haired person one of the Ross family? These bones were turned over to the Wayne County Morgue.

Little Sloss Cemetery was located at Mason Street at Monroe in an old churchyard. It too was "vacated" and the bodies and stones relocated to Northview cemetery in 1915.

In 1946 when arsenal buildings on Garrison Street were being razed, a skull was unearthed. The workers and the police could not find any more bones to go with the skull. A local resident

Andy Palmer who was buying the bricks to build a restaurant at Warren and Telegraph, showed the skull to a doctor. The doctor felt it was an Indian and said that the skull showed signs that its owner suffered sinus troubles. It is believed that Andy Palmer took away the skull for reburial elsewhere.

The Crouch (or Chrouch) Family cemetery on Grindley Park between Oxford and Princeton was still extant in the early 1920s. There was a beaten-down wrought iron fence around it. The entire cemetery was only about 36' x 70' and the surrounding property included some weather-beaten tombstones, an obelisk, a one-and-a-half story frame house, a 20'x30'barn with a loft for hay, a chicken house and apple and peach trees. The Crouches were well known in days past, and the street was named Crouch Street at the time. The Crouch family moved out of the area by about 1910, with only a few folks left behind who had not the interest nor the financial means to undertake the task of vacating their family cemetery.

In 1927, a resident who was just a little boy when the bodies were being dug up remembered the crowd that had gathered. "Oh, yes, it was something I will never forget," he said. "We lived on Academy and we used to take our cow all the way to Telegraph Road and leave her for the day to graze. All of us kids then went to the spot and were watching the workers digging holes and one of them set a skull on top the pile of dirt. He was still in the hole trying to get out the rest of the bones. I think he did that to scare us. And boy, were we scared." The Crouch family members' bodies were dug up at the new land owner's expense and most were reburied in Romulus, Michigan.

Undertaker Elba Howe wrote in his diary that he was hired to go to the "grounds of the powder magazine" to dig up the remains of "the Hitchcock child." The little girl, who died in 1844, may have been the daughter of a soldier or laborer stationed at the Dearbornville Arsenal one block west. Her remains were placed in Northview. The powder magazine and its property would have made an ideal burial ground. It was on a high sand ridge just outside the village proper. Were there any other unrecorded burials that took place on the powder magazine property? The building was sold off by the government about 1875 and was bought and refurbished into the McFadden-Ross House by the Ross family. This building is now a part of the holdings of the Dearborn Historical Museum.

Some people may wonder whatever happened to little Christian Bohn. He was the grandson of early resident Charles Bonatz. The boy died in 1871 at age five and was lovingly buried on his grandfather's land outside the door of the farmhouse. This property is now Dartmouth and Andover Street near Bailey Street in Dearborn Heights. A rather expensive coffin was purchased for him, and the funeral service at his grandfather's residence was well-attended. Was the little boy's grave placed among other family member graves? Was his the only one on Grandpa Bonatz' farm? Most of the Bohns and Bonatzes now rest in Oak Grove Cemetery in Taylor, but there is no marker for Christian. Were his remains removed to a more suitable place when the farm was sold and subdivided, or do they still rest in the earth under someone's driveway or front lawn?

When the old buildings of Conrad Ten Eyck's Tavern were being razed and graded to accommodate the widening of Michigan Avenue, workers discovered a skeleton. This area was on Michigan Avenue west of Southfield Road. The tavern, built in 1826, was a landmark. It had been the first sign of hospitality in the wilderness to pioneers who landed in Detroit and struck out on Michigan Avenue, called the Chicago Road, for their newly purchased farms. It was reported that the skeleton that was found was in a sitting position, which would make it likely a Native American who perished and was buried there, maybe decades before Ten Eyck built his tavern.

The road workers reported that they reburied it nearby, in an undisclosed location, to allow the bones to rest in peace.

The Reves-Wilhelm Cemetery, now in the boundaries of the city of Melvindale at Wall and Homestead Streets was a part of the large farm purchased by Peter Wilhelm in 1827. Mr. Wilhelm emigrated from Germany with his family, and was probably the first burial, as he drowned in the Rouge River shortly after settling on the land. Over the years more of the Wilhelm family was buried there, and in 1885 an obelisk was erected in the center of the cemetery, memorializing the family. When the last family member, Elizabeth Wilhelm Reves died in 1899, her heirs divided up the property and sold it off. The little 4-acre cemetery stayed in the family's control, but was neglected and overgrown. With a low iron gate around it and one very prominent obelisk in the center, it was vandalized, and somewhat forgotten. Just before being plowed over for subdivision developments in 1948, a Reves descendant stepped in and got the site cleaned up and well-marked and in 1963 a Michigan Historical marker was placed there. This cemetery is considered the oldest one outside the City of Detroit to be still in its original location. Many members of the Reves and Wilhelm families rest there and it is estimated that there could be as many as 30 burials there, most unmarked. What destruction that bulldozer and other machinery would have wrought had they turned over the earth of 100-year-old graves and obliterated that little pioneer cemetery.

In the Township of Redford on the Grand River Road in 1889, a man digging post holes for his employer was shocked to discover the skeleton of a human being buried on the land. James Ryan, working on the post holes for William Houghton, had struck something with his auger that stopped his progress. When he examined and dug into the hole a little more, he found the skeleton, and not only that, this skeleton was wearing manacles. Every gawker and onlooker had a theory as to who the unfortunate might have been and how he may have come to be buried there. The manacles, a kind of restraint similar to handcuffs, were of the kind that were old-fashioned even for 1889. The bones of the arms lay there on the ground, still wearing the iron manacles, as folks speculated on the case.

Mr. Houghton, the landowner, guessed that the body had been buried there at least fifty years judging by the age and rusted condition of the chains. About a week after the discovery, a theory about the skeleton was proposed. Almost 53 years earlier, a horse thief was caught in Brownstown. Horse-thieving then was a serious and contemptible crime. The man who was arrested had been caught red-handed in possession of a stolen horse. Since it was late in the day, he was taken by the constable and a posse of settlers to a blacksmith who fashioned the manacles. However, an associate of the thief daringly rode up with another horse and called to his friend to mount up. "Can you ride with your hands like that?" he called to the prisoner. He replied, while jumping onto the horse's back, "By God, I will!" He rode off before anyone could think to pursue him, and he was never re-captured. This prisoner could have made his way north to the place in Redford where the skeleton was found, although this is not very likely. But that scenario illustrates how a manacled man could disappear from the face of the earth and his body re-appear decades later.

At that time, although the Grand River Road was well traveled, that area of Redford Township was heavily wooded and the grounds undisturbed. If he was an escaped prisoner, then it was likely that he died of exposure or starvation, and was buried later by puzzled citizens who found his remains. The Redford skeleton was probably an army deserter or a criminal who may have been executed there and buried.

The most interesting thing is that there is no record of what happened to him next. The land owner turned the skeleton over to the "authorities." So where did the hapless manacled skeleton end up?

Sometimes skeletons turn up in the least likely of places and are neither victims of exposure, starvation, disease or suicide. Such was the case in Taylor in 1858. A farmer's dog found the skeleton of a man in the woods near what is now Eureka and Allen. There were several items near the body that led the authorities to identify the man as an employee of the railroad who was making his way west to Chicago. When his family in Georgia was contacted, they reported that they had not heard from the man, but that his traveling companion, a "Mr. Kennedy" had written letters to them. Kennedy told the family that they had parted ways and the man had gone to Ireland. The traveling companion who wrote the letters assured the family that their loved one would contact them soon.

Eventually Kennedy was found and arrested for the robbery and murder of the railroad man.

When is a burial not a burial? The answer is when the body is stored in a temporary underground chamber. The Nowlin cemetery on Van Born in Dearborn Heights used to have an underground vault for holding bodies before burial. Undertakers took advantage of this space and stored bodies there while the families were nailing down the details of the burial. Sometimes bodies stored in Nowlin's vault were never meant to be buried there permanently and were finally laid to rest in Putnam Cemetery in Taylor. Undertakers could only keep a body so long on the premises of the deceased's home or at the undertaker's rooms before decomposition would make this scenario extremely unsanitary and repulsive. The Nowlin vault is still there but it has been dismantled and caved in. The vault at Northview Cemetery was also built underground and was cool and secure. In later years it functioned as a tool shed according to the owner, until it too was dismantled and a larger caretaker's office and garage were constructed.

No bodies of smallpox victims were allowed to be held in a vault. They were to be buried immediately. And so even after the establishment of community cemeteries with paid caretakers and stockholders, many smallpox victims were buried unceremoniously and quickly on their own property. Many of these kinds of graves may not have been forgotten by their families, but they also were never disturbed as the spread of smallpox was so feared. How many lie to this day still undiscovered in the city's neighborhoods?

The Thomas family burying ground is also called The Old Hill. This was located where Fairlane East and Oakwood Commons are now. In this early photo from Arlene Thomas Davis, taken near the Thomas home, the cemetery is in the background up on the hill. There are no known records of the graves being moved. It is presumed they were obliterated during the construction of the buildings and roads and the straightening of the Rouge River project in the 1960s.

When Cherry Hill Road east of Outer Drive was being graded down for home building endeavors, bits of skeletons and artifacts were found and were presumed to be Native Americans. Henry Ford was in the process of building homes near River Lane when these discoveries were made. Probably all of these items were reburied nearby without much fanfare.

Mount Kelley cemetery in Dearborn, a Catholic cemetery, fell victim to urban sprawl. When Cherry Hill west of Outer Drive was widened several times over the years, bodies that lay in unrecorded and in unidentified graves were left in place and Cherry Hill was paved over it.

In the east end of Dearborn, this was the case at the cemetery churchyard of St. Alphonsus on Warren and Gould. The cemetery has a State Historical Marker. It was established in 1876 but the earliest burials were from the 1840s. The graves of all that could be found nearest to Warren and Schaefer Roads were moved north and east into the churchyard about 1876. Schaefer Road was subsequently paved and then widened over the years and it is no secret that several unidentified graves still lie beneath northbound Schaefer Road.

Also in the east end of town, east of Greenfield south of Michigan Avenue was the Chovin family cemetery. When Henry Ford bought the property, he directed that all the bodies that could be found be reburied in Northview Cemetery. Ford certainly had the financial resources to undertake this task. There is a monument at Northview Cemetery to these re-burials. The Chovin farms were subdivided and sold. The Ford Motor Company, residential neighborhoods and businesses now occupy the areas.

The "Old Hill" cemetery, roughly where Oakwood Commons residential apartments are located, was one of the oldest in the area, predating 1800s. The Thomas Family used this cemetery, which was near their home. The hill was sandy and very prominent. No one knows when it was destroyed, or if there was a search made for forgotten burials.

Imagine how far in one century's time, from 1800 to 1900, the settlements changed with massive progress in manufacturing and transportation alone. In 1800, when a funeral was held, services at the graveside were attended by family, friends and neighbors. By 1900, some of the larger established cemeteries in the Detroit area recorded 1,000 burials per year. Meanwhile, many unofficial burial sites from the 1800s became neighborhoods and parks; tamed, graded, paved and filled in to satisfy the needs of the populace and the incredible progress of urban growth.

This was the vault at Northview Cemetery.

The grave of early resident Lucy Tompkins is shown. She was claimed from Little Sloss Cemetery on Monroe and re-interred in Northview. These photos show the condition of her stone when it was newer and how it appears today.

The End